KATE HALE

Setting Boundaries Between Work and Home

Keeping Personal and Professional Lives Separate

Copyright © 2024 by KATE HALE

All rights reserved. No part of this publication may be reproduced, stored or transmitted in any form or by any means, electronic, mechanical, photocopying, recording, scanning, or otherwise without written permission from the publisher. It is illegal to copy this book, post it to a website, or distribute it by any other means without permission.

First edition

This book was professionally typeset on Reedsy.
Find out more at reedsy.com

Contents

Introduction	1
Recognizing the Signs of Imbalance	4
Establishing Your Boundaries	9
Communicating Boundaries Effectively	14
Time Management Techniques to Reinforce Boundaries	21
Technology and Digital Boundaries	27
Physical Boundaries	34
Mental and Emotional Boundaries	40
Navigating Boundaries in Remote Work	48
Overcoming Challenges and Boundary Breakers	54
Strengthening Your Boundaries Over Time	61
Real-Life Stories of Successful Boundaries	67
Conclusion	76

Introduction

In a world where professional and personal lives are increasingly intertwined, understanding the importance of boundaries has never been more critical. Setting clear boundaries between work and home is not just about compartmentalizing tasks; it is about preserving mental, emotional, and physical well-being. It is about defining when work stops and personal life begins, establishing a sense of control over one's life, and protecting the sanctity of both professional success and personal fulfillment. As remote work becomes more common and digital communication permeates all hours of the day, the challenge of maintaining a healthy separation between work and home life is more pronounced.

Why Setting Boundaries Matters in Modern Work Culture

Modern work culture has evolved rapidly, driven by technological advancements, economic pressures, and shifting societal norms. The result is a culture where constant connectivity and the expectation of always being "on" have blurred the lines between professional responsibilities and personal downtime. Employers, colleagues, and even clients are no longer limited by traditional working hours; the availability of mobile devices, collaboration tools, and instant messaging platforms means that the workday can easily extend into evenings, weekends, and even vacations.

Setting boundaries in this context matters because it safeguards against burnout and fatigue. When the separation between work and home dissolves, stress accumulates, and individuals find themselves in a perpetual state of vigilance. The consequences extend beyond physical exhaustion; emotional well-being and personal relationships also suffer. Work stress bleeds into personal interactions, leading to irritability, lack of focus, and diminished enjoyment of activities outside of work. By establishing clear boundaries, individuals can reclaim their time, energy, and mental clarity, ultimately enhancing their productivity and satisfaction in both spheres of life.

Moreover, boundaries play a pivotal role in defining professionalism and self-respect. When individuals do not set limits on work demands, they send a message—consciously or unconsciously—that their personal time is not valuable. This can lead to increased pressure from managers or colleagues to continually sacrifice personal needs in favor of work demands. Conversely, when clear boundaries are in place, they communicate a strong sense of self-worth and establish a framework for mutual respect.

Understanding Work-Life Balance: A Myth or Reality?

The concept of work-life balance has been a buzzword for decades, yet its feasibility is often questioned. Is achieving a perfect balance truly possible, or is it an elusive ideal? To answer this, it is essential to redefine what balance actually means.

For many, work-life balance evokes an image of evenly divided time and energy between work and personal life. However, this rigid definition fails to account for the fluidity of life and the ever-changing nature of professional and personal demands. Rather than aiming for a perfect 50-50 split, balance should be viewed as a dynamic state of alignment, where one's priorities and boundaries are adjusted based on evolving circumstances.

Achieving work-life balance, therefore, is less about creating equal distribution and more about understanding and honoring what matters most at a given moment. For instance, there may be periods when work takes

INTRODUCTION

precedence due to an important project or career milestone. During these times, work hours may increase temporarily, and personal activities may need to be adjusted. Conversely, when family or personal well-being requires attention, work obligations should be re-evaluated to prioritize these areas.

Acknowledging the myth of perfect balance enables individuals to approach boundary-setting with greater flexibility and realism. It also empowers them to recognize that balance is not a destination but an ongoing process. Rather than feeling guilt or pressure to meet an unrealistic standard, individuals can focus on maintaining harmony between work and home in a way that aligns with their values and goals.

In conclusion, the importance of boundaries in modern work culture cannot be overstated. They are essential not only for preventing burnout and stress but also for fostering healthy relationships and sustaining long-term professional success. By redefining work-life balance and setting clear, realistic boundaries, individuals can create a more fulfilling and sustainable lifestyle.

Recognizing the Signs of Imbalance

The challenge of maintaining boundaries between work and personal life is often not immediately apparent. However, as pressures and responsibilities increase, the subtle merging of professional obligations into personal time can lead to an array of adverse effects. Recognizing the signs of an imbalance is crucial to addressing the issue before it develops into a more severe problem.

Warning Signs of Blurred Boundaries

The first and perhaps most overlooked indicator of imbalance is the consistent overlap of work into non-working hours. With the increasing prevalence of remote work, it has become alarmingly easy to extend the workday beyond traditional hours. While this might seem harmless or even productive in the short term, it erodes the clear demarcation between work and home life. If you find yourself frequently responding to emails late at night, taking calls during family dinners, or working on weekends without clear reasons, these are clear indicators that boundaries are being compromised.

Another common sign of blurred boundaries is an inability to disconnect mentally from work. Even after stepping away from the desk or signing off for the day, lingering thoughts of unfinished tasks, upcoming meetings, or deadlines can pervade your personal time. This mental intrusion is not just a minor inconvenience; it indicates that the mind is unable to rest, which is critical for psychological well-being.

Physical symptoms also often accompany blurred boundaries. If an individual is experiencing frequent headaches, muscle tension, or unexplained fatigue, it might be a signal of underlying stress. These symptoms can be exacerbated by working from home, where there is no physical separation between the environment associated with work and the one meant for relaxation and recovery.

Blurred boundaries also manifest as a pervasive sense of guilt or pressure when not working. If taking time off or engaging in personal activities is accompanied by feelings of guilt, it suggests that work has begun to dominate your self-worth. This can lead to a cycle where you constantly feel the need to prove your dedication to work, even at the expense of your personal time and well-being.

How to Identify Burnout and Its Effects

When boundaries are consistently blurred, the result is often burnout. Burnout is a state of chronic physical and emotional exhaustion, typically accompanied by feelings of cynicism, detachment from work, and a reduced sense of accomplishment. Recognizing the signs of burnout is essential to prevent it from escalating into a serious issue.

One of the earliest signs of burnout is the gradual loss of motivation and enthusiasm for work. Tasks that once felt fulfilling or challenging may begin to feel overwhelming or tedious. You may find yourself dreading the start of each workday or feeling indifferent toward accomplishments that previously brought you satisfaction. This loss of motivation is not just a matter of temporary disinterest; it indicates that work is no longer a source of engagement or purpose.

Another clear sign of burnout is a marked decline in productivity and efficiency. Even when you put in long hours, the quality and quantity of your work may suffer. Simple tasks may take longer to complete, and mistakes become more frequent. This decline in performance can further exacerbate feelings of frustration and inadequacy, creating a self-reinforcing cycle of negativity.

Emotional symptoms are also prevalent in burnout. These can include feelings of hopelessness, irritability, or frequent mood swings. You may find yourself becoming increasingly impatient with colleagues, family members, or even yourself. Emotional exhaustion often leads to withdrawal from both professional and personal relationships, as you struggle to find the energy to engage with others.

Burnout also manifests in physical symptoms. Chronic fatigue, insomnia, frequent illness, and a general sense of being "worn out" are all common indicators. When left unaddressed, these symptoms can lead to more serious health problems, including hypertension, cardiovascular issues, and mental health disorders such as anxiety and depression.

A particularly insidious effect of burnout is the development of a sense of detachment or cynicism toward work. This is characterized by a lack of trust in colleagues, increased skepticism toward organizational goals, or feelings of alienation from one's professional identity. Detachment can be a defense mechanism, as it allows you to distance yourself emotionally from a source of stress. However, over time, it can lead to a complete disconnection from your career and ambitions.

Recognizing these signs of burnout is crucial, as it allows you to take proactive steps toward recovery. Rather than waiting for burnout to reach a crisis point, early identification and intervention can prevent long-term damage to both your personal and professional life.

The Impact on Personal Relationships and Well-being

When work begins to infiltrate your personal life, the consequences are not limited to your professional performance; they can also extend to your personal relationships and overall well-being. One of the most common effects is a gradual erosion of personal connections. As work demands encroach on time that would otherwise be spent with family and friends, these relationships often suffer. This might manifest as missed family events, skipped social gatherings, or a general withdrawal from loved ones due to a lack of time or energy.

The strain on personal relationships can be particularly damaging in close partnerships, such as marriages or long-term relationships. When one partner is consistently preoccupied with work, the other may feel neglected or undervalued. Over time, this can lead to resentment, communication breakdowns, and a sense of emotional distance. In some cases, it may even contribute to the breakdown of the relationship itself.

Even friendships and social circles are not immune to the effects of blurred boundaries. When work takes precedence over social commitments, it sends a message to friends that they are not a priority. Over time, this can result in feelings of isolation and loneliness, as the social connections that are crucial for emotional support begin to weaken.

Another critical aspect of well-being that is impacted by blurred boundaries is self-care. When work dominates your schedule and mental space, activities that are essential for physical and emotional health—such as exercise, hobbies, and relaxation—are often neglected. Over time, this neglect can contribute to a decline in overall health, both physically and mentally.

The lack of separation between work and home can also lead to a loss of personal identity. When work becomes the primary focus of your life, it can be easy to lose sight of who you are outside of your professional role. This can lead to feelings of emptiness or a lack of fulfillment, even when you are successful in your career. A strong sense of identity is crucial for well-being, as it provides a foundation for self-worth and resilience.

Mental health is also deeply affected by blurred boundaries and the resulting imbalance. Chronic stress from overwork can contribute to the development of anxiety disorders, depression, and other mental health issues. When personal time is compromised, there is less opportunity to engage in activities that promote relaxation, joy, and connection—activities that are essential for maintaining a healthy mind.

Lastly, blurred boundaries can lead to a distorted perception of success and self-worth. In a culture that often equates long hours and constant availability with dedication, it can be tempting to measure your worth by your professional achievements. However, this mindset can be detrimental, as it places all of your self-esteem in the hands of your career. When setbacks or challenges inevitably arise at work, they can have a disproportionate impact on your sense of self-worth and happiness.

Understanding the impact of blurred boundaries on personal relationships and well-being is critical to taking corrective action. When these areas of life are compromised, the effects can be far-reaching and long-lasting. Addressing the issue requires a holistic approach that considers not only professional obligations but also personal values, needs, and aspirations.

Recognizing the signs of imbalance is the first step toward reclaiming control over your life and creating a healthier separation between work and home. By being vigilant about these warning signs and their effects, you can take proactive steps to restore balance, protect your well-being, and nurture your relationships.

Establishing Your Boundaries

Establishing boundaries between work and home is not merely an act of setting limits; it is a process of defining your values, clarifying your priorities, and asserting control over your time and energy. The complexity of modern work culture, with its emphasis on constant availability and high productivity, requires a deliberate and proactive approach to creating and maintaining boundaries. This chapter will delve into how you can establish your boundaries effectively by understanding what boundaries mean to you, setting clear boundaries with yourself, and identifying and managing the common boundary breakers.

Defining What Boundaries Mean to You

Before establishing boundaries, it is essential to first understand what boundaries mean in the context of your life. Boundaries are personal guidelines, rules, or limits that you create to identify reasonable, safe, and permissible ways for others to behave towards you and how you will respond when those limits are breached. They are a reflection of your values and what you consider important in balancing your personal and professional lives. Thus, the first step in establishing boundaries is to get clear on what matters most to you.

Start by asking yourself what you want to protect through your boundaries. Is it your family time, your mental health, your personal space, or your ability to recharge after a long day of work? What aspects of your personal life are non-negotiable, and how do you want to be treated in both personal and professional contexts? Understanding these core values will help you define what your boundaries need to be.

For instance, if family time is a priority, you might define a boundary that restricts work-related activities during family dinners or weekends. If mental health is a concern, you might decide that engaging in work tasks beyond a certain hour is off-limits to give your mind time to decompress. By aligning your boundaries with your values, you give them a solid foundation, making it easier to enforce them when challenged.

Another key aspect of defining boundaries is recognizing the difference between physical, emotional, and digital boundaries. Physical boundaries involve your personal space and time, emotional boundaries pertain to your feelings and energy, and digital boundaries deal with the increasing invasion of technology into all aspects of life. Understanding these distinctions allows you to create comprehensive boundaries that address the multiple ways in which work can encroach on your life.

Creating Clear Boundaries with Yourself

Setting boundaries is not only about limiting the behavior of others but also about creating a disciplined approach with yourself. Establishing boundaries with yourself is crucial because, often, the most persistent violator of boundaries is not others but you. Self-imposed pressure to exceed expectations, meet deadlines, and prove dedication can erode the boundaries you set in place.

One effective way to create clear boundaries with yourself is to establish routines and rituals that define when and how work begins and ends. For instance, having a morning routine that includes activities unrelated to work—such as exercise, meditation, or reading—helps you start the day on your terms rather than diving straight into work tasks. Similarly, creating an evening ritual, like a 15-minute wind-down with a book or a walk outside, signals to your brain that the workday is over.

Another essential aspect of creating boundaries with yourself is mastering time management. Allocating specific blocks of time for work tasks, personal activities, and leisure can help prevent the overflow of work into personal time. When you schedule time intentionally, you're more likely to respect the boundaries you set and less likely to feel the need to keep working indefinitely. This is particularly critical in remote work scenarios, where there is no clear delineation between the office and home.

Self-boundaries also extend to the management of technology. Establishing limits on screen time, notifications, and the use of work-related apps outside of working hours is crucial to maintaining mental and emotional boundaries. For instance, turning off work email notifications after a certain hour or muting work chat channels on weekends can help reinforce the separation between work and home.

To successfully create clear boundaries with yourself, self-awareness and self-discipline are key. This means being aware of your tendencies to over commit or sacrifice your well-being for work and taking proactive measures to mitigate these tendencies. It also means acknowledging that establishing boundaries is an ongoing practice rather than a one-time decision. Regularly revisiting and adjusting your boundaries based on changing circumstances and new insights is essential for sustaining them over the long term.

Recognizing and Resisting Boundary Breakers

Even the most well-defined boundaries will inevitably face challenges from various sources. These boundary breakers can come in the form of colleagues, managers, family members, or even the culture of your organization. Being able to recognize these boundary breakers and respond effectively is crucial to maintaining your boundaries.

One of the most common boundary breakers is the expectation of constant availability. In many work environments, there is an unspoken pressure to respond to emails, messages, or calls outside of working hours, perpetuating the myth that productivity and dedication require constant connectivity. This expectation often arises from organizational norms or the behavior of others who model 24/7 availability. However, it is crucial to understand that boundary violations by others are often a reflection of their lack of boundaries rather than your responsibilities.

To resist this pressure, it is essential to communicate your boundaries assertively and consistently. This could mean informing colleagues or managers that you are unavailable for work-related tasks after a certain hour, setting up automated responses that communicate your availability, or scheduling "do not disturb" periods on your calendar. Clarity and consistency in communication reduce misunderstandings and set clear expectations for others regarding your boundaries.

Another common boundary breaker is guilt. When you set boundaries, you may experience guilt for prioritizing your needs over work demands, especially in environments that value overwork or martyrdom. It is important to recognize that guilt is not an indication of wrongdoing but a reflection of the internalized beliefs you hold about work and self-worth. Resisting guilt requires a mindset shift that prioritizes long-term well-being over short-term compliance. Reminding yourself that boundaries are not selfish but necessary for sustained success and happiness can help alleviate guilt and reinforce your resolve.

Family and friends can also inadvertently act as boundary breakers, especially when they are unaware of the pressures you face or when your home is also your workplace. Addressing this requires open and honest communication with loved ones about your boundaries and the reasons behind them. Letting family members know when you are unavailable due to work or when you need uninterrupted focus time helps establish mutual respect for each other's needs.

Finally, recognizing organizational or cultural boundary breakers is essential. In some workplaces, overworking or constant availability is normalized or even glorified. If this is the case, resisting boundary-breaking may require you to challenge the culture or norms of your organization. This can be particularly challenging, as it involves standing up to collective expectations. However, resisting such cultural pressures is crucial if you are to maintain your boundaries and protect your well-being. This could involve having conversations with your manager about workload expectations, seeking support from like-minded colleagues, or exploring opportunities for change within your organization.

Establishing boundaries between work and home is a multifaceted process that requires defining what boundaries mean to you, setting clear limits with yourself, and recognizing and resisting the inevitable challenges to those boundaries. By taking a proactive approach to these elements, you can create a healthier and more fulfilling balance between your professional and personal lives.

Communicating Boundaries Effectively

Setting and maintaining boundaries between work and home is not just a personal exercise; it requires effective communication with the people in your life. Whether it is family, friends, bosses, or colleagues, effectively expressing your boundaries is key to ensuring that they are respected and honored. However, this is easier said than done. Miscommunications, unspoken expectations, and the discomfort of asserting oneself can all complicate the process of setting boundaries. This chapter explores how to communicate your boundaries effectively to family and friends, in the workplace, and how to handle any resistance you may encounter.

Setting Boundaries with Family and Friends

Family and friends are an integral part of your support system, but they can sometimes inadvertently blur the lines between personal and professional life. They may not fully understand the demands of your job, or they may have expectations that conflict with your work commitments. Therefore, setting clear boundaries with them is essential for maintaining a healthy balance between your responsibilities and relationships.

The first step in setting boundaries with family and friends is to communicate your needs and reasons behind them. Clarity is crucial in helping them understand what you are trying to achieve and why it matters to you. For example, if you need uninterrupted time for work or self-care, clearly

COMMUNICATING BOUNDARIES EFFECTIVELY

explaining the impact that interruptions have on your focus, productivity, or well-being can help them understand your perspective. This approach invites them into the conversation rather than making them feel excluded or marginalized.

When communicating boundaries, specificity matters. Vague statements like "I need more time to focus on work" or "Please don't disturb me during the day" can leave room for interpretation and misunderstanding. Instead, try to be precise about when and why you need certain boundaries in place. For instance, you might say, "From 9 AM to 1 PM, I will be working without breaks. Please avoid calling me unless it's urgent," or, "I need an hour of quiet time each evening to unwind, so I won't be answering messages during that time."

It is also important to communicate these boundaries proactively rather than waiting until an issue arises. Anticipating potential conflicts and addressing them in advance demonstrates respect for the relationship and reduces the likelihood of misunderstandings. For instance, if you are planning to work from home and need uninterrupted focus, let your family or roommates know about your work hours and the importance of minimizing disruptions.

However, even with clear communication, setting boundaries with family and friends can be challenging due to the emotional dynamics involved. Loved ones may feel hurt or rejected if they interpret your boundaries as a lack of interest in spending time with them. Therefore, it's essential to emphasize that setting boundaries is not about pushing people away, but about creating a healthier balance between work and personal time. Reassuring them that quality time together is a priority can help them accept and respect your boundaries more easily.

In addition to setting boundaries verbally, it is helpful to reinforce them through actions. If you establish a rule that evenings are reserved for family time, make sure to consistently adhere to it. Your actions should align with your words, as consistency builds trust and reinforces the validity of your boundaries.

How to Communicate Boundaries to Your Boss and Colleagues

Communicating boundaries in the workplace presents its own set of challenges. In professional settings, there is often a power dynamic at play, as well as an expectation of compliance and dedication. However, it is crucial to assert your boundaries in order to avoid burnout, preserve your well-being, and maintain long-term productivity.

When communicating boundaries to your boss, it is important to frame your conversation in a way that emphasizes the mutual benefits. Rather than presenting boundaries as a refusal or limitation, position them as measures that will help you be more effective in your role. For example, instead of saying, "I can't work overtime anymore," try framing it as, "To maintain my productivity and avoid burnout, I need to keep my work hours consistent. This will help me deliver my best work during regular hours."

It is also helpful to come prepared with specific solutions or alternatives when setting boundaries with your boss. For instance, if you need to limit after-hours communication, you could propose alternatives such as prioritizing urgent tasks during the day or setting up regular check-ins to address ongoing concerns. This approach demonstrates that you are committed to finding solutions that benefit both you and the organization.

When setting boundaries with colleagues, transparency and collaboration are key. It can be helpful to openly discuss your working preferences and ask about theirs as well. For instance, you might say, "I've found that my productivity is highest when I can focus without interruptions. Could we set up a time each day to touch base, so we don't need to disrupt each other during work hours?" By framing the conversation as a collaborative effort, you create an environment of mutual respect and understanding.

However, even with careful framing and proactive communication, it is essential to be prepared for potential push back from both your boss and colleagues. Some workplace cultures may prioritize constant availability or overworking, making it difficult to establish boundaries without facing resistance. In these cases, it's essential to be firm in your boundaries while remaining professional and open to dialogue. Reiterate the reasons behind your boundaries and the benefits they provide for both you and the organization.

Additionally, document any discussions or agreements regarding your boundaries. Having a record of these conversations can serve as a reference point if any conflicts or misunderstandings arise in the future. It also demonstrates that you are taking your boundaries seriously and have made an effort to communicate them clearly.

Responding to Push back on Your Boundaries

It is common to encounter push back when setting boundaries, especially in environments or relationships where those boundaries have not previously existed. Push back can come in various forms, from subtle guilt-tripping to direct resistance or attempts to undermine your boundaries. How you respond to this push back plays a significant role in whether your boundaries are ultimately respected or not.

When faced with push back, the first and most important step is to stay calm and composed. Reacting emotionally to resistance can escalate the situation and lead to misunderstandings or conflicts. Instead, take a deep breath, listen to the other person's concerns, and respond with empathy. For example, if a colleague expresses frustration about not being able to reach you after hours, you might acknowledge their feelings by saying, "I understand that it can be inconvenient, and I appreciate your understanding of my need to maintain work-life balance."

It's also essential to remain firm in your boundaries while being open to compromise where appropriate. Compromise does not mean abandoning your boundaries, but rather finding solutions that work for both parties. For instance, if your boss insists on after-hours availability, you could propose a compromise where you check your email once in the evening for urgent matters, while maintaining your boundary of not responding to non-urgent communications.

When push back is persistent or aggressive, assertiveness becomes crucial. Being assertive does not mean being confrontational or defensive; it simply means standing up for your boundaries with confidence and clarity. Reiterate your boundaries calmly and respectfully, and avoid justifying or over-explaining yourself. For example, if someone repeatedly questions why you won't work weekends, a simple and firm response like, "I've set aside weekends for rest and personal time, which allows me to be more focused and effective during the workweek," is sufficient.

It's also helpful to establish consequences for repeated violations of your boundaries. This is particularly relevant in situations where push back comes from colleagues or supervisors who continue to disregard your limits despite clear communication. While consequences should be appropriate to the context and delivered professionally, they demonstrate that you are serious about maintaining your boundaries. For instance, if a colleague continues to call you after hours despite multiple requests not to, you might let them know that you will not be answering calls outside of designated work hours in the future.

In family and personal relationships, push back often comes in the form of guilt or passive-aggressive behavior. For example, a family member might express disappointment or make sarcastic remarks when you prioritize work or self-care over a social commitment. In these cases, it's important to address the underlying emotions behind their push back while reaffirming your boundaries. You might say, "I can see that you're upset, and I value our time together. However, I need to honor my commitments and take care of myself, so I'm not available during that time."

When dealing with guilt-inducing push back, it's crucial to remind yourself that your boundaries are valid and necessary. Guilt is a natural emotional response, but it should not dictate your actions or lead you to compromise your well-being. Take a moment to reflect on why you set your boundaries in the first place and remind yourself of the benefits they provide for you and your relationships.

Finally, remember that not everyone will immediately accept or respect your boundaries, and that's okay. Setting boundaries is about asserting your needs and protecting your well-being, not about seeking approval or validation from others. Accept that push back is a normal part of the process and stay committed to your boundaries, even when it feels uncomfortable.

In conclusion, effectively communicating boundaries requires clarity, confidence, and a proactive approach. By setting clear expectations with family and friends, framing conversations constructively in the workplace, and responding to push back with empathy and firmness, you can establish and maintain boundaries that protect your well-being and support your personal and professional goals. The key is to approach each conversation with a combination of empathy, assertiveness, and consistency.

In setting boundaries with family and friends, it's about making sure they understand your needs without feeling pushed away. Emphasizing the importance of your boundaries for your overall well-being and ability to be present in the time you do spend together can foster understanding and support from your loved ones. Being consistent with your actions reinforces the boundaries you've communicated and builds trust over time.

When communicating with your boss and colleagues, focus on framing boundaries in a way that highlights the mutual benefits and productivity gains. Be clear about what you need, and come prepared with alternatives or compromises that address their concerns. Transparency, proactive planning, and consistency can help create an environment of respect for your boundaries at work.

Responding to push back effectively involves staying calm, being assertive, and resisting guilt or pressure. Acknowledging the other person's perspective while standing firm in your decisions shows that you value the relationship but also prioritize your well-being. Establishing consequences for repeated violations and understanding that not everyone will immediately accept your boundaries helps you stay committed even when faced with resistance.

Ultimately, effective boundary communication is about maintaining healthy and respectful relationships with both yourself and others. It empowers you to take control of your time, energy, and mental space, leading to a more balanced and fulfilling life. By taking a proactive and intentional approach to communicating boundaries, you create the foundation for healthier interactions and long-term well-being in all areas of your life.

Time Management Techniques to Reinforce Boundaries

In a world where demands on our time are increasingly complex and overlapping, time management plays a crucial role in maintaining the boundaries we set between work and personal life. Effective time management is more than simply organizing tasks; it involves a conscious effort to prioritize, structure, and protect your time in a way that aligns with your boundaries and values. This chapter will explore how to harness the power of a daily routine, strategies for prioritizing tasks, and the art of learning to say no without guilt.

The Power of a Daily Routine

One of the most powerful tools for reinforcing boundaries is a well-structured daily routine. A routine not only provides structure and predictability to your day but also serves as a mental cue for when work begins and ends, and when personal or relaxation time starts. Establishing a consistent routine helps minimize the risk of letting work bleed into your personal life and vice versa.

The benefits of a daily routine are multifaceted. First, it creates a rhythm that allows your mind and body to function optimally. When you wake up, start working, take breaks, and wind down at roughly the same times each day, you help regulate your circadian rhythms, which boosts your energy and focus. This predictability can be particularly valuable when working from home, where the lines between work and home life are easily blurred. By setting clear start and stop times for your work, you create a clear boundary between work hours and personal time.

A morning routine is particularly important in setting the tone for the rest of your day. Establishing rituals, such as a short exercise session, journalism, or quiet time with a cup of coffee, helps you mentally prepare for the day ahead and creates a buffer between waking up and diving straight into work-related tasks. These simple acts of self-care can help set a positive tone for your day and establish a clear distinction between your personal time and your professional responsibilities.

Equally important is having a wind-down routine in the evening. This can involve activities like reading, taking a walk, or engaging in a hobby that helps you transition from work mode to relaxation mode. By consistently ending your day with these activities, you signal to your brain that work is over and it's time to relax. This mental shift is crucial for reducing stress and preventing burnout.

However, creating a routine isn't just about allocating specific times for tasks. It's also about identifying your peak productivity hours and structuring your day accordingly. For example, if you are most productive in the morning, schedule your most challenging tasks for that time, and reserve less demanding activities for the afternoon. This alignment between your routine and your natural energy levels helps you accomplish more in less time, reinforcing your boundaries and allowing you to leave work behind when the day is done.

In addition to reinforcing work-life boundaries, a routine can also enhance your ability to disconnect from technology and distractions. Setting designated times for checking emails, responding to messages, and engaging in social media can prevent these activities from encroaching on your work and personal time. By sticking to these digital boundaries, you protect your mental space and maintain a sense of control over your time.

Strategies for Prioritizing Tasks

A key aspect of effective time management and boundary setting is the ability to prioritize tasks. Without clear prioritization, it's easy to become overwhelmed by the sheer volume of demands on your time and to lose sight of what truly matters. Establishing clear priorities helps you focus on high-impact activities and avoid getting caught up in low-priority tasks that can drain your energy and infringe on your personal time.

One of the most effective methods for prioritizing tasks is the Eisenhower Matrix, which categorizes tasks into four quadrants based on their urgency and importance. This matrix encourages you to focus on tasks that are both important and urgent, delegate or postpone tasks that are less urgent, and eliminate tasks that are neither urgent nor important. By regularly evaluating your tasks using this framework, you gain clarity on where to direct your energy and attention.

Another helpful strategy for prioritizing tasks is the "ABC Method." This method involves labeling tasks as "A," "B," or "C" based on their level of importance, with "A" tasks being the highest priority. Within each category, you can then further rank tasks numerically (e.g., A1, A2, B1, B2). This method provides a clear visual representation of what needs to be done first, which can prevent procrastination and ensure that you tackle high-priority items without getting sidetracked by less critical activities.

It's also crucial to regularly revisit and adjust your priorities as new information and tasks arise. Life is dynamic, and your priorities will inevitably change as circumstances evolve. Scheduling regular time each week to review and update your to-do list allows you to stay proactive rather than reactive, giving you greater control over your time and boundaries.

One of the most overlooked aspects of prioritization is recognizing that not all tasks need to be completed by you personally. Delegating tasks to others or outsourcing certain responsibilities can free up valuable time for high-priority activities. For instance, if a task is time-consuming but not central to your core responsibilities, consider delegating it to a colleague or hiring external help. Delegation is not a sign of weakness but rather an acknowledgment that your time and energy are finite resources that need to be protected.

Lastly, a critical part of prioritizing tasks is setting limits on how much you take on. Over committing is a common boundary breaker that often stems from a desire to please others or prove your worth. However, taking on too many responsibilities can lead to burnout and compromise your ability to uphold your boundaries. Learning to prioritize and limit your commitments is essential for maintaining balance and protecting your well-being.

Learning to Say No Without Guilt

Saying no is one of the most challenging yet essential skills for reinforcing boundaries. Many people struggle with saying no due to a fear of disappointing others, damaging relationships, or appearing uncooperative. However, consistently saying yes to every request not only undermines your boundaries but also leads to burnout and resentment.

The first step in learning to say no is to re-frame your understanding of what it means to set boundaries. Saying no is not about rejecting others or being selfish; it's about protecting your time, energy, and priorities. By saying no to tasks or commitments that do not align with your values or goals, you are actually saying yes to what matters most to you. This shift in perspective can help alleviate some of the guilt associated with saying no.

It's also important to recognize that saying no doesn't have to be harsh or confrontational. There are various ways to decline requests while still being respectful and considerate. For example, you can use the "soft no," which involves expressing appreciation for the offer and then politely declining. Phrasing like, "Thank you for thinking of me, but I'm unable to take this on right now," or "I appreciate the opportunity, but my schedule is full at the moment," conveys your decision while maintaining a positive tone.

Another approach is the "conditional no," where you offer an alternative or compromise. For instance, if a colleague asks you to take on an additional project, you could respond with, "I'm currently focused on other priorities, but I can help review the project once the initial draft is ready." This approach shows that you are still willing to contribute within the confines of your boundaries.

When saying no to social invitations or personal requests, honesty is often the best policy. If you need time to recharge or focus on personal commitments, it's okay to let others know. For instance, you might say, "I've had a busy week and need some downtime to recharge, so I won't be able to make it to the event, but I appreciate the invite." Being honest about your needs not only reinforces your boundaries but also encourages others to respect and support them.

It's natural to feel guilty when saying no, especially if you are someone who values helping others or being perceived as dependable. However, it's essential to recognize that guilt is a feeling, not a fact. Just because you feel guilty doesn't mean you are doing something wrong. Practice self-compassion and remind yourself that setting boundaries is necessary for your well-being and long-term success. Over time, as you continue to say no in alignment with your values, the guilt will diminish, and your confidence in your decisions will grow.

Lastly, it's essential to remember that saying no is not a one-time event but an ongoing practice. There will always be new requests, opportunities, and challenges that test your boundaries. By regularly reflecting on your values, priorities, and limits, you can continue to refine your ability to say no without guilt and reinforce your boundaries effectively.

In conclusion, time management techniques such as establishing a daily routine, prioritizing tasks, and learning to say no are powerful tools for reinforcing boundaries. A consistent routine creates predictability and structure, while effective prioritization helps you focus on what truly matters. Learning to say no without guilt allows you to protect your time and energy without compromising your well-being. By mastering these techniques, you can create a balanced and fulfilling life that honors both your professional and personal commitments.

Technology and Digital Boundaries

The modern work environment is dominated by technology that blurs the lines between personal and professional life. Smartphones, work apps, and social media have made it easier than ever to stay connected, but this constant connectivity can come at a cost. Without clear boundaries, technology can encroach on our personal lives, leading to stress, burnout, and a diminished sense of well-being. Managing digital boundaries effectively is essential for maintaining a balanced life and protecting your mental space. This chapter explores practical strategies for managing notifications and work apps, establishing digital detox practices, and separating personal and professional digital spaces.

Managing Notifications and Work Apps

One of the primary sources of digital intrusion into personal life is the constant stream of notifications from work apps and communication tools. Email alerts, instant messaging apps, social media notifications, and calendar reminders can disrupt focus, relaxation, and personal interactions, making it difficult to disconnect from work. The first step in creating digital boundaries is to take control of your notifications.

A practical approach to managing notifications is to assess which notifications are essential and which ones are merely distractions. Start by identifying the apps that require real-time attention and those that do not. For example, while messages from your manager or team might warrant immediate attention during work hours, notifications from social media or non-essential apps can be silenced. Take advantage of your phone's and computer's notification settings to disable non-urgent notifications or set specific times when notifications are allowed. By limiting interruptions, you can concentrate more effectively on your work and personal activities.

Another strategy is to use "Do Not Disturb" (DND) modes or scheduled downtime features available on most devices. Setting your phone or computer to DND mode during focus periods or after work hours can help maintain a separation between work and personal time. For example, you can schedule DND to activate automatically in the evening to avoid being disturbed by work emails or messages during your personal time.

In addition to managing notifications, setting specific hours for checking work apps is essential. For instance, you might decide to check your work email twice a day—in the morning and mid-afternoon—rather than constantly monitoring it throughout the day. This strategy, known as "batch processing," minimizes interruptions and allows you to address communications more efficiently. By establishing designated times for checking work apps, you create a sense of control over your digital interactions, preventing them from encroaching on your personal time.

Managing notifications is also about setting clear expectations with colleagues and managers. It's essential to communicate your availability and digital boundaries so that others understand when it's appropriate to contact you and when you are offline. For example, you might include your work hours in your email signature or set up automated responses that indicate when you are unavailable. Clear communication reduces misunderstandings and encourages a culture of respect for digital boundaries.

While it's important to manage notifications during work hours, it's equally crucial to disconnect completely during your personal time. Turning off work apps and notifications after a certain hour each day signals to your brain that work is over and it's time to unwind. Consistently disconnecting in this way helps prevent burnout and promotes a healthier balance between work and personal life.

Establishing Digital Detox Practices

In a world where technology is omnipresent, taking regular breaks from digital devices is essential for maintaining mental and emotional well-being. A digital detox involves intentionally disconnecting from screens and devices to recharge, reset, and refocus. Establishing digital detox practices can help you regain control over your digital habits and reinforce your boundaries.

One effective digital detox practice is setting aside "tech-free" times or days. For example, you might designate Sunday mornings as a time to disconnect from all screens and instead engage in activities such as reading, spending time outdoors, or enjoying a hobby. Alternatively, you can establish tech-free hours each evening, such as avoiding screens for one hour before bed. These periods of intentional disconnection allow your brain to rest and recharge, reducing the mental fatigue that comes from constant digital engagement.

It's also helpful to identify activities that can replace screen time during your digital detox. Engaging in physical activities, socializing face-to-face, pursuing creative hobbies, or practicing mindfulness exercises can provide a refreshing break from technology. By filling your tech-free time with meaningful activities, you're more likely to stick to your digital detox and reap the benefits of reduced screen exposure.

Another aspect of digital detoxing is being mindful of how you use social media. Social media platforms are designed to capture and hold your attention, often at the expense of your time and mental well-being. To establish healthier boundaries with social media, consider setting limits on your usage. Most smartphones now offer built-in screen time tracking and app usage limits, allowing you to set daily time limits for social media apps.

By monitoring and limiting your social media usage, you reduce the risk of mindless scrolling and create more space for activities that contribute to your well-being.

In addition to setting limits, consider taking periodic breaks from social media altogether. A "social media fast," where you temporarily deactivate your accounts or delete the apps from your phone for a set period, can help you reset your relationship with these platforms. Many people find that stepping away from social media for a few days or weeks helps them gain perspective and clarity, as well as reduces feelings of comparison and FOMO (fear of missing out).

For those who rely heavily on digital devices for work, it's also crucial to create physical spaces in your home that are tech-free. For instance, designating the dining table, bedroom, or living room as no-phone zones can help reinforce boundaries and encourage more meaningful interactions with family and friends. By intentionally creating tech-free spaces, you signal to yourself and others that these areas are meant for relaxation and connection, not digital distractions.

Establishing digital detox practices is not about completely eliminating technology but rather about using it mindfully and purposefully. Regular digital detoxes allow you to step back, reset, and approach your digital interactions with greater intention and awareness. This practice reinforces your boundaries and helps you maintain a healthier balance between online and offline life.

Separating Personal and Professional Digital Spaces

One of the challenges of modern work life is the merging of personal and professional digital spaces. With the rise of remote work and the proliferation of digital communication tools, it's common for personal and work-related messages, emails, and apps to coexist on the same devices. This overlap can make it difficult to disconnect from work and maintain clear boundaries. Separating your personal and professional digital spaces is essential for preserving your mental space and preventing burnout.

A practical way to achieve this separation is to create dedicated digital environments for work and personal activities. For instance, consider using separate devices for work and personal use. If you have a work laptop or phone, limit work-related activities to those devices and reserve your personal phone or computer for non-work tasks. This physical separation of devices creates a clear boundary and reduces the temptation to check work emails or apps during your personal time.

If using separate devices isn't feasible, you can still create distinct digital environments by organizing your apps and accounts. For example, you can set up different user profiles on your computer for work and personal use, with each profile having its own set of apps, bookmarks, and preferences. Similarly, consider using separate email addresses for work and personal communications to keep your inboxes organized and reduce the risk of work-related emails spilling into your personal time.

In addition to organizing your digital spaces, it's helpful to establish digital rituals that signal the start and end of your workday. For example, at the beginning of your workday, you might open your work-related apps and tools, and at the end of the day, close them all and switch to your personal profile or environment. These small actions create a mental distinction between work and personal time, helping you transition more smoothly between the two.

Another aspect of separating personal and professional digital spaces is managing your communication channels. Work communication tools like Slack, Microsoft Teams, or Zoom can easily spill over into personal time if not managed properly. One strategy is to turn off work-related notifications outside of work hours or to set clear expectations with colleagues about your availability. For instance, you might let your team know that you won't be

SETTING BOUNDARIES BETWEEN WORK AND HOME

responding to messages after 6 PM or that you will only be available for emergencies during weekends.

It's also important to communicate your boundaries with family and friends regarding work-related digital interactions. For instance, if family members frequently reach out to you for work-related help or advice, let them know when you are available to assist and when you are off-duty. Establishing these boundaries helps protect your personal time and prevents work-related issues from encroaching on your relaxation and downtime.

Another valuable strategy is to minimize the overlap between work and personal apps by using separate tools or platforms for each. For example, consider using different messaging apps for work and personal communications, such as using WhatsApp for personal chats and Microsoft Teams for work discussions. This separation allows you to maintain a clear distinction between work and personal interactions and reduces the likelihood of being drawn into work-related conversations during your personal time.

For those who work from home, creating a designated workspace can also reinforce digital boundaries. Having a specific area in your home where you conduct work tasks helps signal to your brain that work is confined to that space. When you leave your workspace, it becomes easier to switch off mentally and engage in personal activities. This physical separation between work and personal spaces can significantly reduce the sense of being "always on" and promote a healthier work-life balance.

Separating personal and professional digital spaces is ultimately about creating clear distinctions between work and personal life in your digital environment. By taking intentional steps to organize your devices, apps, and communication channels, you can regain control over your digital interactions and reinforce your boundaries.

In conclusion, managing digital boundaries requires a combination of practical strategies and mindful practices. By taking control of notifications, establishing regular digital detoxes, and separating personal and professional digital spaces, you can protect your time, energy, and mental well-being. These strategies not only reinforce your boundaries but also promote a healthier and more balanced relationship with technology.

In today's interconnected world, the temptation to stay constantly plugged in is stronger than ever. However, creating and maintaining digital boundaries is essential for preserving your well-being, productivity, and the quality of your personal life. By taking a proactive approach to managing notifications and work apps, you can reduce distractions and regain control over when and how you engage with your digital environment. Establishing digital detox practices provides necessary breaks from the screen and helps you reconnect with the world offline. Finally, separating personal and professional digital spaces allows you to create clearer mental and physical distinctions between work and home life, reinforcing your boundaries and promoting balance.

As you continue to navigate the complexities of technology in your personal and professional life, remember that digital boundaries are not fixed or one-size-fits-all. They require ongoing assessment and adjustment based on your needs, responsibilities, and values. Stay mindful of how your digital habits impact your time, relationships, and mental health, and don't hesitate to make changes as needed.

By implementing these strategies, you can cultivate a healthier relationship with technology and create a more intentional, fulfilling life where your time and attention are truly your own.

Physical Boundaries

The concept of physical boundaries often extends beyond the mere arrangement of walls and doors; it encompasses the creation of dedicated spaces that align with your needs for productivity, relaxation, and mental clarity. As the lines between home and work have blurred, especially with the rise of remote work, establishing physical boundaries within your home has become crucial. When spaces are intentionally designed, they not only reinforce mental and emotional boundaries but also foster a sense of order and balance. In this chapter, we explore how to design a home office for focus, set up your home for relaxation, and understand the significance of transition rituals in maintaining these physical boundaries.

Designing a Home Office for Focus

A dedicated workspace is a vital component of maintaining physical boundaries between work and personal life. Whether you have an entire room to spare or just a corner, creating a space that supports focus and productivity can significantly impact your ability to concentrate and disconnect when the workday is over. The goal is to design an environment that signals to your brain that it's time to work, minimizing distractions and promoting mental clarity.

When designing a home office, the first consideration is location. Ideally, your workspace should be in a quiet area away from high-traffic zones and common distractions like the television, kitchen, or family activities. If possible, choose a room with a door that can be closed to create a clear separation between your work environment and the rest of your home. A closed door serves as a physical barrier to interruptions and helps signal to others that you are in "work mode."

Once you've chosen a location, the next step is to furnish your home office with essentials that promote focus and comfort. A supportive chair and an ergonomic desk setup are critical for maintaining good posture and preventing physical discomfort, which can be a major distraction during long work hours. Position your desk near a window if possible, as natural light has been shown to boost mood and productivity. However, be mindful of glare and reflections that could interfere with your screen visibility.

Beyond furniture, consider the aesthetic and sensory elements of your workspace. Cluttered environments can contribute to stress and distraction, so aim for a minimalist setup with only the essentials within arm's reach. Adding plants, artwork, or personal items that inspire you can create a more inviting and motivating space. Additionally, consider the color palette of your workspace; colors like blue and green are often associated with calm and focus, while bright colors like red or orange can be energizing but potentially overstimulating.

Technology setup is another crucial aspect of a home office. Ensure that your workspace is equipped with all necessary tools and equipment, such as a reliable computer, high-speed internet connection, noise-canceling headphones, and office supplies. Minimizing the need to leave your workspace frequently for supplies or tech issues helps maintain a consistent flow of work and reduces interruptions.

Lastly, define clear working hours and physical boundaries for your workspace. When you enter your home office, treat it as if you are arriving at a traditional office. Resist the temptation to use this space for non-work activities, such as watching videos or socializing online, as this can blur the mental association between your workspace and focus. At the end of the workday, close your laptop, turn off the lights, and physically leave the room, signaling to yourself that the workday is complete. This separation helps reinforce the boundary between work and home, making it easier to switch off mentally and engage in personal activities.

Setting Up Your Home for Relaxation

Just as it is essential to have a dedicated workspace, it is equally important to create spaces within your home that are designed for relaxation and unwinding. Your home should be a sanctuary where you can recharge and disconnect from the demands of work. By intentionally setting up areas that promote relaxation, you create physical boundaries that encourage rest and mental rejuvenation.

The first step in setting up your home for relaxation is to identify which areas are meant for rest and leisure. The bedroom, living room, and outdoor spaces like a balcony or garden are natural candidates for relaxation zones. Once these areas are identified, focus on optimizing them for comfort and tranquility.

In the bedroom, prioritize creating a sleep-friendly environment. Invest in a quality mattress and pillows that support restful sleep, and use blackout curtains or eye masks to block out external light. Keep the bedroom free from work-related clutter, electronics, and distractions that could interfere with sleep quality. Ideally, your bedroom should be a place where you can completely disconnect from work-related stress and focus solely on rest and relaxation.

For the living room or relaxation area, consider how you can create a comfortable and inviting space for unwinding. Cozy furniture, soft lighting, and elements like blankets, cushions, and throws can help create a sense of warmth and comfort. Arrange the furniture to encourage conversation, relaxation, or entertainment, and avoid placing work-related items like laptops or paperwork in this space. This separation reinforces the boundary between work and leisure, allowing you to fully disconnect during downtime.

If you have access to outdoor spaces like a balcony, garden, or patio, take advantage of them to create a nature-inspired retreat. Spending time outdoors has been shown to reduce stress and improve mood, so consider setting up a small seating area where you can enjoy fresh air, sunlight, and greenery. Adding elements like potted plants, a hammock, or a comfortable chair can transform even a small outdoor space into a relaxing escape.

Music and scent are also powerful tools for creating a relaxing atmosphere. Soft background music, ambient sounds, or nature recordings can help create a calming environment and drown out intrusive noise. Similarly, using essential oils or scented candles with relaxing scents like lavender or chamomile can contribute to a sense of tranquility. These sensory elements can help signal to your brain that it's time to relax, enhancing your ability to disconnect from work stress.

In addition to creating designated relaxation spaces, it's important to establish ground rules for how these areas are used. For example, you might decide that the living room is a no-work zone after 6 PM, or that the bedroom is reserved solely for rest and sleep. By setting clear boundaries for how these spaces are used, you create physical and mental cues that reinforce the distinction between work and relaxation.

The Importance of Transition Rituals

One of the challenges of working from home is the absence of a physical commute, which traditionally serves as a transition between work and home life. Without this built-in transition, it can be difficult to mentally switch gears, leading to a sense of always being "on" and never fully disconnecting.

SETTING BOUNDARIES BETWEEN WORK AND HOME

This is where transition rituals come into play. Transition rituals are intentional actions or routines that help signal to your brain that one part of the day is ending and another is beginning. By establishing transition rituals, you create a psychological boundary that separates work time from personal time.

A common and effective transition ritual is taking a short walk at the end of the workday. Going for a walk serves as a physical and mental break, giving you a chance to decompress, clear your mind, and release the stress of the day. Walking also provides a change of scenery and a sense of movement, simulating the effect of a commute. When you return home, you're more likely to feel refreshed and ready to engage in personal activities.

Another simple transition ritual is changing your clothes at the end of the workday. Just as you would dress differently for the office and for relaxing at home, changing into casual clothes can help signal to your brain that the workday is over. This physical change reinforces the separation between your professional and personal life, making it easier to switch off from work mode.

Engaging in brief mindfulness practices or meditation sessions can also be an effective transition ritual. Taking just five to ten minutes to focus on your breathing, practice gratitude, or reflect on the day can help clear your mind and release lingering work-related thoughts. These moments of mindfulness create a buffer between work and home, reducing stress and improving your ability to be present in your personal life.

For those who enjoy cooking, preparing a meal at the end of the day can serve as a therapeutic transition ritual. Cooking involves tactile engagement and creativity, which can help shift your focus away from work-related concerns. Additionally, the process of preparing and sharing a meal with family or friends reinforces the importance of personal connections and downtime.

If you have specific hobbies or interests, incorporating them into your transition ritual can also be beneficial. Whether it's playing a musical instrument, working on a puzzle, practicing yoga, or reading a book, engaging in activities you enjoy creates a mental and emotional shift that reinforces the separation between work and home.

Incorporating these transition rituals consistently helps create a rhythm to your day, reducing the mental load and promoting a sense of balance. Transition rituals are especially important in preventing work-related stress from carrying over into your personal time, which can impact your relationships and overall well-being.

Creating and maintaining physical boundaries through dedicated spaces, intentional relaxation zones, and transition rituals is essential for preserving your well-being in a world where work and home life increasingly overlap. By designing a home office that supports focus, setting up your home to encourage relaxation, and establishing rituals that signal the end of the workday, you can reinforce the boundaries between your professional and personal life.

Ultimately, these physical boundaries are not just about managing space; they are about creating an environment that aligns with your values and priorities, supporting your ability to focus, relax, and connect with yourself and others. Through intentional design and mindful practices, you can cultivate a home environment that promotes balance, well-being, and fulfillment.

Mental and Emotional Boundaries

Mental and emotional boundaries are essential for protecting one's well-being, especially in a world where work demands, personal relationships, and external pressures constantly intersect. Unlike physical boundaries, which are more tangible, mental and emotional boundaries require a deeper understanding of one's inner state and an ability to regulate emotions effectively. Establishing these boundaries is crucial for preventing stress, avoiding burnout, and maintaining a healthy sense of self. This chapter delves into strategies for managing stress and anxiety from work, cultivating emotional detachment, and reinforcing boundaries through mindfulness practices.

Managing Stress and Anxiety from Work

Stress and anxiety are common responses to the pressures of work. They manifest not only in the form of physical symptoms like headaches, fatigue, and insomnia but also through mental and emotional signs such as worry, irritability, and a sense of overwhelm. While some degree of stress can be motivating, chronic stress and unchecked anxiety can erode mental boundaries, leading to burnout and diminishing your ability to disconnect from work.

One of the first steps in managing stress and anxiety from work is identifying the specific sources of stress. This requires self-awareness and reflection to pinpoint the triggers that consistently lead to feelings of tension or unease.

Common stressors might include heavy workloads, tight deadlines, difficult colleagues, or unclear expectations. Once identified, these triggers can be addressed through proactive strategies such as delegation, time management, and effective communication.

In addition to identifying stressors, it is crucial to set realistic expectations for yourself. Over committing or striving for perfection in every task can lead to feelings of inadequacy and exhaustion. Learning to set achievable goals and recognize your limitations can help alleviate the pressure you place on yourself. This might involve prioritizing tasks based on their urgency and importance, delegating responsibilities, or simply acknowledging that it's okay to make mistakes.

Another key strategy for managing stress and anxiety is establishing clear work boundaries, both physically and mentally. This involves defining your work hours and creating a designated workspace that separates your professional and personal life. However, it's equally important to set mental boundaries by consciously limiting the amount of time and energy you devote to work-related thoughts outside of those hours. This might mean resisting the urge to check emails in the evening or avoiding work discussions during personal time.

Exercise and physical activity are also powerful tools for managing stress. Regular physical activity releases endorphins, which can elevate your mood and reduce feelings of anxiety. Whether it's going for a run, practicing yoga, or taking a walk during breaks, incorporating movement into your daily routine can help clear your mind and improve your ability to handle stress. Additionally, physical activity provides a healthy outlet for releasing built-up tension and energy.

Breathing exercises and progressive muscle relaxation techniques can also be effective for alleviating stress. Deep, diaphragmatic breathing helps activate the parasympathetic nervous system, which is responsible for promoting relaxation and reducing the body's stress response. Similarly, progressive muscle relaxation involves systematically tensing and relaxing different muscle groups to release physical tension and calm the mind.

Lastly, it's essential to have a strong support system in place. Sharing your concerns with a trusted friend, family member, or mentor can provide relief and perspective. Sometimes, simply expressing your feelings and receiving empathy can help reduce the emotional burden of stress. Additionally, seeking professional support from a therapist or counselor can offer valuable tools and techniques for managing anxiety more effectively.

Emotional Detachment Strategies

Emotional detachment is the ability to create a psychological distance between yourself and emotionally charged situations or relationships. This does not mean becoming indifferent or callous but rather learning to protect your emotional energy and avoid becoming overly entangled in others' emotions or work-related stress. When emotional boundaries are weak, you may find yourself taking on others' problems, feeling responsible for their emotions, or becoming overly invested in work situations that are beyond your control.

One of the most effective strategies for cultivating emotional detachment is practicing self-reflection and self-awareness. This involves recognizing when you are becoming overly emotionally involved in a situation and taking a step back to evaluate your role. For instance, if you find yourself feeling overwhelmed by a colleague's negativity or constantly worrying about a project's outcome, pause and ask yourself whether this level of emotional investment is necessary or helpful. By acknowledging your emotions and their triggers, you gain greater control over how you respond.

Setting clear boundaries around emotional involvement also requires recognizing that you cannot control others' feelings or fix their problems. When colleagues or loved ones are going through challenges, it's natural to want to help or provide support. However, taking on their emotional burdens can lead to feelings of exhaustion and resentment. Instead, offer empathy and support without taking responsibility for their emotions. This might mean listening actively, expressing compassion, and offering solutions when appropriate, but also recognizing when it's necessary to step back and let others manage their own emotions.

Another aspect of emotional detachment is avoiding rationalization. Rationalization is the tendency to take responsibility for or blame oneself for external events or others' reactions. For instance, if a colleague responds negatively to feedback or if a project doesn't go as planned, it's easy to internalize these outcomes as a reflection of your worth or competence. However, learning to separate your self-worth from external events helps you maintain emotional resilience and reduces the likelihood of becoming overwhelmed by situations beyond your control.

One effective technique for emotional detachment is re-framing your perspective. This involves consciously shifting your mindset to view situations in a more objective or neutral light. For example, if a colleague's criticism triggers feelings of insecurity, try to re-frame the criticism as feedback meant to improve your work rather than a personal attack. Re-framing helps you depersonalize situations and maintain a more balanced emotional state.

It's also helpful to practice visualization techniques that reinforce emotional boundaries. Visualization involves mentally creating a barrier or protective space between yourself and external stressors. For instance, you might imagine a clear shield around you that allows you to be present and compassionate but prevents others' emotions from penetrating your emotional space. This mental imagery can be particularly effective in high-stress or emotionally charged environments where maintaining detachment is challenging.

Journalism is another powerful tool for processing and detaching from intense emotions. Writing down your thoughts and feelings allows you to externalize and examine them from a distance. This practice can help you gain perspective, release pent-up emotions, and identify patterns in your emotional responses. Over time, journalism can enhance your self-awareness and reinforce your ability to set and maintain emotional boundaries.

Practicing Mindfulness for Boundary Reinforcement

Mindfulness is the practice of being fully present and aware of your thoughts, feelings, and surroundings without judgment. It involves cultivating a state of focused attention and acceptance, allowing you to respond to situations with greater clarity and intention. When it comes to establishing mental and emotional boundaries, mindfulness can be an invaluable tool for reinforcing those boundaries and enhancing your overall well-being.

One of the primary benefits of mindfulness is its ability to increase self-awareness. By practicing mindfulness, you become more attuned to your internal state and can recognize when your mental or emotional boundaries are being compromised. For example, if you notice yourself ruminating on work-related problems during your personal time, mindfulness allows you to observe these thoughts without becoming entangled in them. This awareness creates the space to consciously choose how you want to respond, whether that means letting go of the thoughts or redirecting your focus.

Mindfulness also helps you stay grounded in the present moment, reducing the tendency to dwell on past mistakes or worry about future outcomes. By staying present, you can approach situations with a clearer mind and avoid becoming overwhelmed by negative emotions. This is particularly helpful when dealing with stressful work situations or emotionally charged interactions, as it allows you to respond thoughtfully rather than react impulsively.

Incorporating mindfulness practices into your daily routine can strengthen your mental and emotional boundaries over time. One simple practice is mindful breathing, which involves paying close attention to your breath as it moves in and out of your body. When you notice your mind wandering to work-related worries or emotional stressors, gently bring your focus back to your breath. This practice not only calms your nervous system but also reinforces your ability to redirect your attention away from intrusive thoughts.

Body scan meditation is another mindfulness technique that can help reinforce boundaries. This practice involves mentally scanning your body from head to toe, noticing any areas of tension or discomfort without trying to change them. By bringing awareness to physical sensations, you create a deeper connection between your mind and body, which can help release stress and strengthen your sense of self-awareness.

Another effective mindfulness practice is loving-kindness meditation, which involves silently repeating phrases of goodwill and compassion toward yourself and others. For example, you might repeat phrases such as, "May I be happy. May I be healthy. May I be at peace." Practicing loving-kindness meditation helps cultivate self-compassion and reinforces the understanding that setting boundaries is an act of self-care, not selfishness.

In addition to formal meditation practices, mindfulness can be integrated into everyday activities. For instance, you can practice mindful eating by fully engaging your senses as you eat, noticing the taste, texture, and aroma of each bite. Similarly, you can practice mindfulness while walking, focusing on the sensation of your feet touching the ground and the movement of your body. These simple practices help cultivate a state of mindfulness that carries over into other areas of your life, reinforcing your boundaries and enhancing your ability to stay present.

Mindfulness also encourages acceptance and non-judgment, which are crucial for maintaining emotional boundaries. When you practice mindfulness, you learn to accept your emotions without trying to suppress or control them. This acceptance allows you to experience emotions fully without becoming overwhelmed or losing your sense of self. For example, if you feel anger or frustration in response to a work-related conflict, mindfulness enables you to acknowledge the emotion without letting it dictate your actions or reactions.

In conclusion, mental and emotional boundaries are essential for protecting your well-being and maintaining balance in a demanding world. By managing stress and anxiety from work, cultivating emotional detachment, and practicing mindfulness, you can establish and reinforce these boundaries effectively. These strategies not only help you manage external pressures and demands but also cultivate a sense of inner peace and resilience.

Managing stress and anxiety from work involves being proactive about identifying your triggers, setting realistic expectations, and establishing clear boundaries in both physical and mental spaces. By incorporating regular exercise, relaxation techniques, and seeking support when needed, you can better regulate your stress levels and protect your mental and emotional health.

Emotional detachment, on the other hand, is not about distancing yourself from others or becoming indifferent; it's about maintaining a healthy separation between your emotions and external events or people. Through self-awareness, re-framing, and setting clear limits on emotional involvement, you can prevent external pressures from overwhelming your sense of self. Techniques like journalism, visualization, and avoiding rationalization can further strengthen your ability to detach emotionally when needed.

Mindfulness acts as a reinforcing tool for these boundaries, allowing you to cultivate awareness and presence in every moment. Whether through formal meditation, mindful breathing, or integrating mindfulness into daily activities, these practices help you stay grounded, reduce stress, and enhance your capacity to navigate emotionally charged situations with clarity and grace.

Ultimately, by combining these approaches, you can build a robust framework of mental and emotional boundaries that support your well-being, resilience, and ability to engage fully in both your professional and personal life. This proactive and intentional effort to maintain your boundaries will lead to a healthier, more fulfilling existence, where you feel empowered to manage your emotions, focus your attention, and prioritize your inner peace.

Navigating Boundaries in Remote Work

The shift towards remote work has transformed the way many people engage with their professional responsibilities. While working from home offers significant benefits like flexibility and reduced commuting time, it also comes with challenges that can blur the boundaries between work and personal life. Navigating these boundaries requires intentional strategies and practices to ensure a healthy balance. This chapter explores the specific challenges of working from home, building effective boundaries with remote teams and employers, and learning how to switch off when work is always "on."

Challenges of Working from Home

Working from home can create a variety of challenges that are unique compared to traditional office environments. The physical absence of boundaries, such as separate office spaces and defined working hours, makes it easier for work to encroach on personal time. Additionally, the constant presence of work-related technology within the home, combined with the pressure to remain available and productive, can lead to a sense of always being "on."

One of the most common challenges faced by remote workers is the difficulty in separating professional responsibilities from personal obligations. Without the clear distinction of physically leaving the office, work-related tasks can easily spill over into evenings and weekends. This lack of separation can lead to increased stress and a feeling of being overwhelmed by work. Over time, this constant connection to work may result in burnout, reduced productivity, and a diminished quality of life.

Another significant challenge in remote work is managing interruptions and distractions at home. Unlike the structured environment of a traditional office, a home setting is often shared with family members, roommates, or pets, all of whom can unintentionally disrupt your workflow. Even in a quiet home environment, distractions such as household chores, errands, and personal activities can tempt you away from your work tasks. These distractions not only disrupt productivity but can also blur the lines between work and home life.

Remote work can also create feelings of isolation and loneliness, especially for those who thrive on social interaction and collaboration. The absence of face-to-face interactions with colleagues can lead to a sense of disconnection and contribute to feelings of isolation. This challenge can be compounded by a lack of clear communication and the potential for misunderstandings in remote work settings, making it essential to establish boundaries that promote connection without compromising personal space.

Additionally, the pressure to remain constantly available is a prevalent challenge in remote work environments. With digital tools like instant messaging apps, email, and video conferencing, there is often an unspoken expectation to respond immediately, even outside of regular working hours. This pressure can lead to an "always-on" mindset, where employees feel compelled to check messages, respond to emails, and remain connected to work at all times.

Building Boundaries with Remote Teams and Employers

Establishing clear boundaries with remote teams and employers is essential for maintaining a healthy work-life balance. However, doing so requires proactive communication, mutual understanding, and a willingness to prioritize well-being alongside productivity. Building these boundaries begins with setting clear expectations around availability, work hours, and communication practices.

One of the most effective ways to establish boundaries with remote teams is to define and communicate your working hours clearly. Let your team and employer know when you are available for work-related tasks and when you are off-duty. Including your working hours in your email signature, online calendar, or instant messaging status can serve as a gentle reminder to others about your availability. Additionally, setting up automated email responses or status updates during non-working hours can reinforce your boundaries and reduce the likelihood of receiving after-hours requests.

It's also essential to have open conversations with your employer or manager about workload and expectations. Remote work can sometimes create ambiguity around performance metrics and deadlines, leading to an increased workload or unrealistic expectations. Regular check-ins with your manager can provide an opportunity to discuss your capacity, clarify priorities, and set realistic deadlines. Being transparent about your boundaries and workload not only helps prevent burnout but also fosters a culture of trust and mutual respect.

Establishing communication protocols with your remote team is another crucial aspect of building boundaries. Discussing and agreeing on preferred communication methods and response times can help reduce the pressure to be constantly available. For example, you might decide as a team that urgent matters will be communicated via phone calls, while less urgent tasks can be addressed through email with a 24-hour response window. This clarity allows everyone to manage their time more effectively and reduces the anxiety of having to monitor multiple communication channels constantly.

In addition to setting communication protocols, it's important to establish "focus time" within your work schedule. Focus time refers to dedicated periods where you can work without interruptions, allowing you to complete tasks efficiently. Let your team know when your focus time is scheduled, and consider using tools like status updates or shared calendars to indicate when you are unavailable for meetings or non-urgent messages. By establishing and respecting each other's focus time, you create a work environment that values deep work and minimizes unnecessary disruptions.

Another key aspect of building boundaries with remote teams is practicing digital disconnection. This involves setting specific times to turn off work-related devices and log out of work apps at the end of the day. Communicating your disconnection times with your team reinforces the message that you are unavailable during personal hours. While the idea of disconnecting might seem daunting, it ultimately leads to better mental clarity, increased productivity during working hours, and improved well-being.

It's also essential to lead by example and encourage boundary-setting practices within your team. If you are in a leadership or management role, model healthy boundaries by respecting your own work hours and taking regular breaks. Encourage your team members to do the same by promoting a culture that values balance and well-being over constant availability. When employees see that their leaders prioritize boundaries, they are more likely to feel comfortable establishing their own.

How to Switch Off When Work is Always "On"

One of the most challenging aspects of remote work is learning how to switch off when work is always within reach. Without the clear boundaries provided by an office setting and a commute, it can be difficult to mentally and emotionally disconnect from work. However, developing the ability to switch off is essential for preventing burnout and maintaining a sense of well-being.

SETTING BOUNDARIES BETWEEN WORK AND HOME

One effective strategy for switching off is to create a clear end-of-day ritual. Just as a morning routine helps signal the start of the workday, an end-of-day ritual can help signal the transition from work to personal time. This ritual might include closing your laptop, turning off your work notifications, tidying up your workspace, and changing into more comfortable clothes. By consistently practicing this ritual, you create a mental association between these actions and the end of the workday, making it easier to switch off mentally.

Establishing physical boundaries within your home can also support your ability to switch off. Designating a specific area for work, such as a home office or a dedicated corner, helps create a clear separation between work and personal spaces. When you leave your workspace at the end of the day, it reinforces the boundary between work and home life. If you have limited space, consider using visual or physical cues, such as a room divider, a plant, or a specific chair, to mark the transition between work and personal activities.

It's equally important to set boundaries around technology usage in order to switch off effectively. This involves establishing designated times to disconnect from work devices and limit screen time. For example, you might decide to turn off work-related notifications after 6 PM or avoid checking your email on weekends. Additionally, consider using apps or features on your devices that restrict access to work apps during personal hours. By consciously creating these digital boundaries, you can reduce the temptation to stay connected to work at all times.

Another key aspect of switching off is practicing mindful transitions between work and personal time. Mindful transitions involve intentionally pausing and reflecting as you shift from one activity to another. For example, at the end of the workday, you might take a few minutes to practice deep breathing, stretch, or listen to a favorite song. These small actions help signal to your brain that it's time to unwind and switch gears. Over time, these mindful transitions can become powerful cues for disconnecting from work and entering a state of relaxation.

Incorporating physical activity into your end-of-day routine can also help you switch off effectively. Engaging in activities like walking, jogging, cycling, or practicing yoga provides a natural transition from a sedentary workday to more dynamic personal time. Physical movement not only releases tension but also promotes mental clarity and reduces the lingering effects of stress. This transition can be particularly valuable for remote workers who spend long hours sitting at a desk.

It's also essential to create intentional "no-work" times within your schedule. These are periods where you intentionally engage in activities that have nothing to do with work, such as spending time with family, pursuing a hobby, or enjoying leisure activities. By actively scheduling no-work times and treating them as non-negotiable, you reinforce your boundaries and prioritize personal well-being. This intentional disconnection helps create a sense of balance and prevents work from overshadowing other aspects of your life.

Finally, if switching off remains a challenge, consider seeking support or accountability from a colleague, friend, or mentor. Share your intention to set boundaries and ask them to check in with you periodically to see how you're doing. Having someone who can offer encouragement and remind you of your goals can be incredibly helpful in reinforcing your commitment to switching off.

In conclusion, navigating boundaries in remote work requires a multifaceted approach that addresses the unique challenges of working from home, builds clear boundaries with remote teams and employers, and cultivates the ability to switch off effectively. By proactively establishing these boundaries and prioritizing your well-being, you can create a healthier and more balanced remote work experience.

Overcoming Challenges and Boundary Breakers

Setting boundaries is a vital part of maintaining personal and professional well-being, but it is only the first step. Even with clear and well-communicated boundaries, there will inevitably be challenges and individuals who attempt to break or undermine them. The key to navigating these situations is not only to recognize when your boundaries are being violated but also to respond effectively and assertively. This chapter explores how to handle boundary violations with grace, recognize manipulative tactics at work, and build resilience and self-advocacy skills to protect your boundaries in the long term.

Handling Boundary Violations with Grace

Boundary violations occur when someone disregards or oversteps the limits you've set, either intentionally or unintentionally. These violations can range from small, seemingly harmless actions to more overt intrusions. When boundaries are breached, it's natural to feel a mix of emotions, such as anger, frustration, or even guilt. However, responding with grace is crucial to maintaining your dignity and the integrity of your relationships.

The first step in handling a boundary violation is to assess the situation calmly before reacting. Take a moment to evaluate whether the violation was intentional or a misunderstanding. Sometimes, people may overstep boundaries without realizing it, especially if those boundaries were not explicitly communicated. In these cases, a gentle reminder can be more effective than an emotional outburst. For example, if a colleague repeatedly interrupts you during focus hours, a simple, calm statement like, "I've scheduled this time to focus, and I would appreciate if we could discuss this after 3 PM," can reinforce your boundary without escalating the situation.

When addressing boundary violations, it's essential to be assertive but not aggressive. Being assertive involves clearly and directly communicating your needs while remaining respectful of the other person. This can be particularly challenging in professional settings where power dynamics come into play. To communicate assertively, use "I" statements that focus on your feelings and needs rather than placing blame. For instance, saying, "I need uninterrupted time in the mornings to complete my work efficiently," is more effective and less confrontational than, "You always interrupt me when I'm trying to work."

It's also helpful to establish consequences for repeated boundary violations. Consequences are not about punishing others but rather about reinforcing the importance of your boundaries and protecting your well-being. For instance, if a team member continues to call you after hours despite being asked not to, you might inform them that you will not be answering non-urgent calls outside of working hours moving forward. Communicating consequences calmly and consistently signals to others that you are serious about maintaining your boundaries.

In cases where boundary violations persist despite clear communication, it may be necessary to escalate the issue. This could involve having a more formal conversation with the person involved, seeking support from a supervisor or HR representative, or establishing written agreements to clarify expectations. When escalating boundary violations, focus on the impact of the behavior on your work or well-being, rather than making it personal. This approach not only maintains professionalism but also increases the likelihood of achieving a constructive resolution.

Recognizing Manipulative Tactics at Work

Manipulative tactics are often subtle and insidious, making them challenging to identify and address. At work, these tactics can manifest in various forms, such as guilt-tripping, gas lighting, or passive-aggressive behavior. When left unchecked, manipulation can erode boundaries, create a toxic work environment, and undermine your confidence. Recognizing these tactics is the first step in protecting your boundaries and taking appropriate action.

Guilt-tripping is one of the most common manipulative tactics used to undermine boundaries. It occurs when someone tries to make you feel guilty for asserting your needs or saying no. For example, a colleague might say, "I thought we were supposed to be a team," or "I guess I'll just have to do it myself if you can't help." These statements are designed to evoke guilt and pressure you into complying with their requests. To counter guilt-tripping, it's essential to acknowledge your feelings of guilt without letting them dictate your actions. Responding with empathy but holding firm to your boundaries can be effective. For example, you might say, "I understand that this is important, but I'm not able to take on additional tasks right now."

Gas lighting is another manipulative tactic that involves making you question your perceptions or memories. In a work context, this might look like a manager denying promises they made or dismissing your concerns as irrational. Gas lighting can be especially damaging to your boundaries because it undermines your confidence in your judgment. If you suspect gas lighting, document interactions and decisions in writing, and seek clarity through direct, factual questions. For instance, if a manager denies agreeing to a deadline extension, you might refer to previous emails or meeting notes as evidence.

Passive-aggressive behavior is another common tactic that can undermine boundaries. This behavior often involves indirect expressions of resentment, such as sarcastic comments, procrastination, or deliberate non-compliance.

Passive-aggressive colleagues might respond to your boundaries with comments like, "Well, if you really need your 'alone time,' I guess I can manage on my own." To address passive-aggressive behavior, it's helpful to confront the issue directly but tactfully. Acknowledge the behavior you've observed and ask for clarity. For example, you might say, "I noticed you seemed upset when I mentioned needing uninterrupted time. Is there something you'd like to discuss?"

Manipulative tactics can also include leveraging authority or seniority to pressure you into compromising your boundaries. For instance, a manager might say, "We all have to make sacrifices to get this project done," implying that declining to work overtime would be unacceptable. In these situations, it's crucial to stand firm in your boundaries while offering alternative solutions. For example, you could respond by saying, "I'm committed to helping the team succeed, but I'm not available for overtime tonight. Let's discuss how I can contribute during my regular hours."

Recognizing manipulative tactics is not always straightforward, as they are often subtle and designed to create confusion or self-doubt. However, by staying aware of your boundaries, trusting your instincts, and seeking clarity in interactions, you can protect yourself from manipulation and maintain a sense of agency.

Building Resilience and Self-Advocacy Skills

Resilience and self-advocacy are essential skills for maintaining boundaries in the face of challenges. Resilience enables you to withstand external pressures and recover from setbacks, while self-advocacy empowers you to assert your needs confidently and effectively. Together, these skills provide a foundation for long-term boundary maintenance and personal well-being.

Building resilience starts with cultivating a strong sense of self-awareness and self-compassion. This involves recognizing and acknowledging your emotions without judgment and responding to yourself with kindness rather than criticism. For example, if you feel guilty for asserting a boundary, instead of berating yourself, practice self-compassion by acknowledging that your needs are valid and that setting boundaries is an act of self-care. Over time, self-compassion strengthens your resilience by reducing the impact of negative emotions and promoting a more balanced perspective.

Another key aspect of resilience is developing a growth mindset. A growth mindset involves viewing challenges and setbacks as opportunities for learning and growth rather than as failures. For example, if a boundary you set was not respected, instead of seeing it as a failure, you could view it as an opportunity to refine your communication skills or reinforce your boundaries more effectively. Adopting this mindset helps you remain adaptable and proactive in the face of boundary-related challenges.

In addition to resilience, self-advocacy is crucial for maintaining boundaries and protecting your well-being. Self-advocacy involves clearly expressing your needs, values, and boundaries while respecting the needs of others. It requires confidence, assertiveness, and a willingness to stand up for yourself even in the face of resistance or push back.

One of the most important self-advocacy skills is assertive communication. This involves speaking clearly, confidently, and directly while maintaining a respectful tone. Assertive communication is not about being aggressive or demanding; rather, it's about expressing your needs in a way that acknowledges the other person's perspective while remaining firm in your boundaries. For example, if a colleague repeatedly interrupts you during meetings, assertive communication might involve saying, "I appreciate your input, but I need to finish my point before we move on."

Another aspect of self-advocacy is developing the ability to say no without guilt. This can be particularly challenging if you are someone who values helping others or if you fear disappointing those around you. However, saying

OVERCOMING CHALLENGES AND BOUNDARY BREAKERS

no is an essential part of protecting your boundaries and preventing burnout. To say no effectively, it's helpful to use clear and direct language, such as, "I'm not able to take on this project right now," rather than offering vague excuses. Practicing saying no in low-stakes situations can help build your confidence for when you need to assert your boundaries in more challenging circumstances.

It's also important to prepare yourself mentally and emotionally for potential push back when advocating for your boundaries. Not everyone will respond positively to your boundaries, and that's okay. Staying firm in your convictions and reminding yourself of the reasons behind your boundaries can help you remain confident in the face of resistance. Having a support system, such as trusted colleagues, friends, or mentors, can also provide encouragement and reinforcement when facing challenges.

Finally, building resilience and self-advocacy involves recognizing and celebrating your progress. Maintaining boundaries is an ongoing practice, and it's important to acknowledge the steps you've taken to protect your well-being. Whether it's successfully asserting a boundary, recognizing a manipulative tactic, or recovering from a boundary violation, taking time to reflect on and appreciate your growth reinforces your commitment to maintaining your boundaries.

In conclusion, overcoming challenges and boundary breakers requires a combination of grace, awareness, and skill. By handling boundary violations with assertiveness and respect, recognizing manipulative tactics, and building resilience and self-advocacy skills, you can navigate these challenges effectively and protect your well-being in both personal and professional environments. These strategies not only strengthen your boundaries but also empower you to maintain a sense of control and balance in your life.

When handling boundary violations, it's crucial to approach situations with a calm and assertive demeanor, focusing on clear communication and setting appropriate consequences if necessary. This proactive approach helps you address issues without escalating conflicts or creating unnecessary tension. Recognizing manipulative tactics, on the other hand, involves being vigilant and self-aware. Understanding how to identify and respond to these tactics protects your boundaries from being eroded by subtle pressure or covert behavior.

Building resilience and self-advocacy skills forms the cornerstone of maintaining boundaries in the long run. Resilience allows you to recover from setbacks and remain steadfast in your commitment to protecting your well-being. Meanwhile, self-advocacy empowers you to express your needs and values confidently, even in challenging circumstances. By combining these skills, you create a framework that supports ongoing personal growth and well-being.

Ultimately, overcoming challenges and boundary breakers requires both inner strength and practical strategies. The journey to maintaining healthy boundaries is not always easy, but it is essential for achieving balance, protecting your mental and emotional health, and cultivating meaningful relationships in both your personal and professional life. By applying the principles in this chapter, you can develop the resilience and confidence needed to navigate obstacles with grace and maintain boundaries that support a fulfilling and balanced life.

Strengthening Your Boundaries Over Time

Writing boundaries is not a one-time task, but an ongoing journey that evolves as life circumstances, relationships, and professional situations change. Effective boundaries require regular reflection, adjustments, and the creation of supportive habits that reinforce these limits over the long term. To maintain healthy boundaries and prevent them from becoming eroded over time, it is essential to revisit and revise them, develop habits that sustain them, and recognize when professional support might be necessary to address persistent challenges.

Revisiting and Revising Boundaries Regularly

Boundaries are not static; they must adapt to new contexts, responsibilities, and challenges. This adaptability is crucial because rigid, unchanging boundaries can become ineffective or counterproductive as your circumstances evolve. Life transitions, such as starting a new job, entering a relationship, becoming a parent, or experiencing a major loss, often require reevaluating existing boundaries to ensure they still align with your needs, values, and well-being.

Revisiting your boundaries regularly involves taking time to reflect on how they are serving you and whether they continue to support your mental, emotional, and physical health. One effective strategy is to conduct a quarterly or biannual review of your boundaries. During this review, ask yourself questions such as:

- Which boundaries have been effective, and which have been challenging to maintain?
    - Are there areas where my boundaries have been crossed or compromised?
    - Have there been significant changes in my life or work that require adjustments to my boundaries?
    - Are there new stressors or demands that have emerged, and how can I address them with revised boundaries?

These questions can help you gain clarity on where adjustments are needed and identify potential weaknesses or areas of overreach in your current boundaries. For instance, if you find that work responsibilities are increasingly spilling over into evenings, it may be necessary to reinforce your work hours more firmly or communicate new availability limits to colleagues.

When revising boundaries, it's essential to communicate changes clearly and proactively. This communication not only prevents misunderstandings but also signals your commitment to maintaining and respecting your boundaries. For example, if you've decided to establish new limits on after-hours communication, inform your team or clients about these changes and explain how it will benefit both your productivity and well-being.

It's also helpful to be flexible in your revisions. Sometimes, boundaries need to be tightened, while at other times, they may need to be relaxed slightly to accommodate new developments. For instance, during a busy season at work, you might allow for occasional overtime while still ensuring that this is an exception rather than the norm. Being adaptable and open to adjustments prevents your boundaries from becoming overly rigid or unrealistic, which can lead to feelings of frustration or failure.

In addition to planned reviews, be mindful of unexpected changes or warning signs that indicate a need to revisit your boundaries. These warning signs might include feeling increasingly stressed, resentful, or exhausted, or noticing that certain individuals consistently push or disregard your boundaries. When these signs arise, take a moment to reflect on what adjustments might be necessary to protect your well-being.

Creating Long-Term Habits for Success

To sustain healthy boundaries over time, it's crucial to develop habits that reinforce and protect them. Habits provide a foundation of consistency and reliability, reducing the mental effort required to maintain boundaries and making them a more natural part of your routine. However, creating long-term habits involves more than just setting intentions; it requires intentional practice, commitment, and patience.

One key habit for maintaining boundaries is to practice assertive communication regularly. Assertiveness is not a skill that comes naturally to everyone, but it can be developed with consistent effort. Practicing assertive communication in low-stakes situations, such as expressing a preference in casual conversations, helps build confidence for more challenging scenarios. Over time, this habit becomes ingrained, making it easier to express your boundaries clearly and effectively when needed.

Another important habit is scheduling regular self-care and downtime. Prioritizing self-care prevents burnout and reinforces the message to yourself and others that your well-being matters. Make it a habit to set aside time each day or week for activities that recharge you, such as exercising, reading, spending time with loved ones, or pursuing hobbies. By consistently carving out personal time, you strengthen your boundaries and create a buffer against external pressures.

Establishing rituals or routines that signal the start and end of work or other activities is another habit that reinforces boundaries. For example, having a morning routine that prepares you for work, and an evening routine that helps you unwind and disconnect, creates clear distinctions between different parts of your day. These rituals serve as mental cues that reinforce your boundaries without requiring constant conscious effort.

Building habits around technology usage is also crucial for maintaining digital boundaries. This might involve setting specific times to check emails, using "Do Not Disturb" features on your devices during personal hours, or implementing a "no phones at the dinner table" rule. These habits help prevent technology from encroaching on your personal time and reinforce the boundary between work and leisure.

In addition to individual habits, it's essential to establish collective habits within your relationships and professional environments. This might involve setting recurring meetings with your manager to discuss workload and expectations, establishing check-ins with family members about personal boundaries, or creating team norms around after-hours communication. These collective habits foster a culture of mutual respect for boundaries and reduce the likelihood of misunderstandings or conflicts.

One effective way to reinforce new habits is to use reminders and accountability tools. For instance, setting reminders on your phone to take breaks, scheduling personal time in your calendar, or enlisting a friend or colleague to check in on your progress can help keep you on track. Over time, as these habits become more ingrained, you'll find that maintaining your boundaries feels less like a conscious effort and more like a natural part of your routine.

When to Seek Professional Support for Boundary Issues

While self-reflection and habit-building can significantly strengthen your boundaries, there may be times when professional support is necessary to address persistent challenges or deeply ingrained patterns. Seeking professional help is not a sign of weakness; rather, it's a proactive step toward gaining the tools and insights needed to protect your well-being more effectively.

One indication that professional support might be needed is if you find yourself consistently struggling to assert or maintain your boundaries despite repeated efforts. This could manifest as an inability to say no, feeling guilty or anxious whenever you set limits, or repeatedly experiencing boundary violations in relationships or work. If these challenges persist, working with a therapist or counselor can provide a safe space to explore underlying beliefs or fears that may be impacting your ability to set and maintain boundaries.

Another sign that professional support may be beneficial is if boundary issues are causing significant stress, anxiety, or emotional distress. For example, if you frequently feel overwhelmed by others' demands, experience chronic feelings of resentment, or struggle with burnout, it may be helpful to seek guidance from a mental health professional. Therapists can offer techniques for managing stress, improving assertiveness, and addressing the emotional impact of boundary challenges.

Professional support is also valuable if you find yourself dealing with manipulative or toxic individuals who consistently undermine your boundaries. In these situations, it's not always easy to recognize or address manipulative behavior on your own. A therapist can help you identify patterns of manipulation, develop strategies for protecting yourself, and build the confidence needed to confront challenging individuals or situations.

For those in leadership or management roles, seeking professional coaching or leadership training can be beneficial for strengthening boundaries in a professional context. Coaching can provide insights into effective communication, delegation, and time management skills, helping you set and maintain boundaries within your team or organization. This not only protects your well-being but also models healthy boundary practices for your team.

SETTING BOUNDARIES BETWEEN WORK AND HOME

In addition to therapy and coaching, there are other forms of professional support that can help strengthen boundaries. For instance, attending workshops or training sessions on assertiveness, conflict resolution, or work-life balance can provide practical tools and techniques. Similarly, joining support groups or communities focused on personal growth or professional development can offer encouragement and accountability as you work to reinforce your boundaries.

It's important to recognize that seeking professional support is not about "fixing" yourself; rather, it's about gaining additional resources and perspectives to navigate complex boundary challenges. Everyone faces difficulties in maintaining boundaries at times, and having access to professional support can make a significant difference in your ability to protect your well-being and achieve long-term success.

In conclusion, strengthening your boundaries over time requires a combination of regular reflection, intentional habit-building, and a willingness to seek support when needed. Revisiting and revising your boundaries allows them to adapt to changing circumstances and ensures they continue to align with your needs and values. Creating long-term habits provides a foundation of consistency and reliability, making it easier to maintain boundaries without constant conscious effort. Finally, recognizing when professional support is necessary empowers you to address persistent challenges and deepen your understanding of yourself and your boundaries.

By embracing this ongoing journey of reflection, adaptation, and growth, you can cultivate boundaries that protect your well-being and support a fulfilling and balanced life.

Real-Life Stories of Successful Boundaries

The concept of setting boundaries between work and personal life is not just theoretical—it is a practice that many people have successfully integrated into their lives to achieve a healthier work-life balance and greater well-being. Learning from the real-life experiences of others provides valuable insights into the challenges and rewards of maintaining boundaries. In this chapter, we will explore case studies of professionals who have taken control of their work-life balance, as well as lessons learned from their failures and adjustments.

Case Studies: Professionals Who Took Control of Their Work-Life Balance

Case Study 1: Emily's Journey to Redefine Her Availability

Emily, a marketing executive at a fast-paced tech company, was known for her dedication to her job. She was always the first to respond to emails, attend meetings, and volunteer for projects. Over time, this level of commitment began to take a toll on her well-being. Emily found herself working late into the evenings and even on weekends, which led to increased stress, exhaustion, and feelings of resentment toward her job.

Realizing that her current approach was unsustainable, Emily decided to take control of her work-life balance by redefining her availability. She began by setting specific work hours and informing her team that she would no longer be checking emails after 6 PM or on weekends, except for urgent matters. To reinforce this boundary, Emily turned off work email notifications on her phone and set up an automated response for after-hours messages.

At first, Emily worried about how her team and manager would react to her new boundaries. However, she communicated her decision with confidence, explaining that it would allow her to be more focused and productive during regular working hours. To her surprise, her team was supportive, and some even followed her lead by setting their own boundaries.

Over time, Emily's decision to redefine her availability resulted in a noticeable improvement in her well-being. She was able to spend more quality time with her family, engage in hobbies she enjoyed, and return to work each day feeling refreshed and energized. Emily's experience demonstrates that taking control of one's availability is not only possible but also beneficial for both personal and professional success.

Case Study 2: Michael's Strategy for Managing Remote Work Distractions

Michael, a software developer, transitioned to remote work during the COVID-19 pandemic. While working from home provided him with flexibility, it also introduced a new set of challenges. With a young child at home, Michael struggled to focus on work tasks due to frequent interruptions and distractions. As a result, his productivity declined, and he began to feel overwhelmed and stressed.

Recognizing that he needed to establish clearer boundaries between work and home life, Michael decided to create a designated home office in a spare bedroom. He communicated with his spouse about his need for uninterrupted focus time and established a signal—a closed door—that indicated he was in work mode. Michael also implemented a routine of taking short breaks to check in with his family, which helped him feel more present and connected.

In addition to creating a physical boundary, Michael set digital boundaries by using a "Do Not Disturb" mode on his phone and computer during focus hours. He informed his team of his designated work hours and encouraged them to schedule meetings during specific windows to minimize disruptions.

By creating both physical and digital boundaries, Michael was able to regain his focus and productivity while maintaining a healthy connection with his family. His experience highlights the importance of establishing clear signals and communication channels to protect one's work environment from distractions.

Case Study 3: Sandra's Journey to Assertive Communication

Sandra, a project manager at a consulting firm, struggled with assertive communication. She often found herself agreeing to take on additional tasks and projects, even when her workload was already full. This pattern of over committing led to burnout and feelings of frustration, as Sandra felt that her contributions were being taken for granted.

To address this issue, Sandra decided to work on developing her assertive communication skills. She attended a workshop on assertiveness, where she learned techniques for expressing her needs and saying no without feeling guilty. Sandra also began practicing these skills in low-stakes situations, such as expressing her preferences in group discussions or setting limits on personal commitments.

When it came time to apply her new skills at work, Sandra felt nervous but determined. During a meeting with her supervisor, she respectfully communicated her current workload and explained that taking on additional projects would compromise the quality of her work. She proposed an alternative solution—prioritizing existing tasks or delegating certain responsibilities to other team members.

Sandra's assertiveness paid off. Her supervisor appreciated her transparency and willingness to find a solution, and Sandra was able to maintain a more manageable workload. Over time, Sandra became more confident in asserting her boundaries, which led to improved well-being and a stronger sense of control over her professional life.

Case Study 4: David's Approach to Balancing Career Ambitions and Family Time

David, a senior executive at a financial services company, was ambitious and driven in his career. However, his relentless pursuit of success often came at the expense of family time. David's wife and children expressed their frustration with his constant work-related absences and lack of engagement during family activities. David knew he needed to make a change, but he struggled with guilt and the fear of falling behind at work.

After a candid conversation with his family, David decided to set clear boundaries around his work schedule. He implemented a "no meetings after 5 PM" rule and designated weekends as family time. David also made a commitment to be fully present during family activities by leaving his phone in another room and resisting the urge to check emails.

To reinforce his boundaries, David communicated his new schedule to his team and set the expectation that non-urgent matters could wait until regular business hours. He also delegated some of his responsibilities to trusted team members, which not only helped lighten his workload but also empowered his colleagues to take on more leadership roles.

David's decision to prioritize family time resulted in stronger relationships with his wife and children, as well as a renewed sense of fulfillment in his personal life. Professionally, he found that his team was capable of handling challenges without his constant oversight, which allowed him to focus on strategic leadership. David's experience demonstrates that balancing career ambitions with family time is achievable with clear boundaries and a commitment to being present.

Lessons Learned from Failures and Adjustments

While successful case studies provide valuable insights, it's equally important to acknowledge that setting and maintaining boundaries is not always a smooth process. There are times when boundaries are tested, compromised, or need to be adjusted in response to changing circumstances. Learning from these challenges is crucial for developing resilience and refining one's approach to boundaries.

Lesson 1: The Importance of Flexibility

One of the key lessons from boundary-related challenges is the need for flexibility. Rigid boundaries that do not account for changing situations or unforeseen events can lead to frustration and resistance. For example, Sandra, the project manager, initially set strict boundaries around her work hours to protect her personal time. However, she soon realized that her role sometimes required flexibility to accommodate urgent client needs or last-minute project changes.

Rather than abandoning her boundaries, Sandra chose to revise them to allow for occasional flexibility while maintaining a core set of non-negotiable limits. She established a "flexible buffer" in her schedule that could be used for urgent tasks, and she communicated this buffer to her team to avoid unnecessary disruptions. This approach allowed Sandra to adapt to changing demands without compromising her overall well-being.

Lesson 2: Learning from Over commitment

Emily's journey to redefine her availability was not without its setbacks. In her initial attempts to set boundaries, she often reverted to old habits of over committing and responding to emails after hours. This pattern led to a cycle of boundary violations, followed by feelings of guilt and self-criticism.

To break this cycle, Emily sought guidance from a mentor who had successfully established boundaries in a similar role. Her mentor encouraged her to practice self-compassion and view boundary setbacks as learning opportunities rather than failures. Emily also began tracking her after-hours work patterns to identify triggers and make proactive adjustments.

By embracing self-compassion and adopting a growth mindset, Emily was able to approach her boundaries with greater patience and resilience. She learned that setbacks are a natural part of the process and that consistency is more important than perfection.

Lesson 3: The Power of Communicating Needs Early

Michael's experience with managing remote work distractions highlighted the importance of communicating needs early rather than waiting until issues escalate. Initially, Michael hesitated to discuss his challenges with his spouse, fearing that it would come across as a lack of commitment to his family. However, as the disruptions continued, Michael's stress levels increased, and his productivity suffered.

After several unproductive workdays, Michael decided to have an open conversation with his spouse about his need for uninterrupted focus time. He explained how setting clear signals, such as a closed door, would benefit both his work and family life. To his relief, his spouse was understanding and supportive, and together they implemented a schedule that balanced Michael's work needs with family time.

Michael's experience illustrates that communicating needs early—before stress and frustration build up—can prevent misunderstandings and create a more supportive environment for maintaining boundaries.

Lesson 4: Recognizing the Need for Professional Support

David's journey to balancing career ambitions and family time was not without challenges. Despite his efforts to prioritize family time, David occasionally found himself slipping back into old habits of checking emails during family activities or working late into the night. He felt conflicted between his desire to succeed professionally and his commitment to his family.

Recognizing that he needed additional support, David sought the guidance of an executive coach who specialized in work-life balance. The coach helped David explore the underlying beliefs and fears that were driving his behavior, such as the fear of missing out on career opportunities. Through coaching, David was able to challenge these beliefs and develop strategies for reinforcing his boundaries more effectively.

David's experience underscores the value of seeking professional support when boundary challenges persist despite repeated efforts. Professional support can provide new perspectives, tools, and strategies that help break longstanding patterns and create lasting change. In David's case, working with a coach enabled him to confront his fears, establish more sustainable boundaries, and achieve a healthier work-life balance.

Lesson 5: Adapting Boundaries to Different Stages of Life

Sandra's assertiveness journey highlighted the importance of adapting boundaries to different life stages. After successfully establishing boundaries at work, Sandra experienced a major life change—she became a new parent. This transition required her to reevaluate her existing boundaries and make adjustments to accommodate her new responsibilities and priorities.

Sandra found that the boundaries she had set before becoming a parent no longer fit her current needs. She needed more flexibility to care for her child while still fulfilling her professional responsibilities. Instead of trying to rigidly adhere to her old boundaries, Sandra worked with her manager to create a modified schedule that allowed her to balance both work and family life.

This experience taught Sandra the importance of regularly revisiting and revising boundaries as life circumstances change. She learned that boundaries are not static rules but dynamic guidelines that should evolve in response to new roles, responsibilities, and priorities.

Lesson 6: The Impact of Cultural Expectations on Boundaries

In some cases, boundary challenges can be influenced by cultural expectations and norms within an organization or community. Michael, the software developer, encountered cultural resistance when he first implemented his focus hours and turned off notifications during those times. Some of his colleagues interpreted his actions as a lack of dedication or accessibility.

Rather than abandoning his boundaries in response to this pressure, Michael chose to address the cultural expectations directly. He initiated a conversation with his manager and team about the importance of uninterrupted focus time for productivity and well-being. He shared research on the benefits of deep work and suggested implementing focus hours as a team-wide practice.

Michael's proactive approach led to a positive cultural shift within his team. His colleagues became more aware of the value of focus time and began adopting similar practices. Michael's experience demonstrates that addressing cultural expectations openly and collaboratively can lead to greater acceptance of boundaries and healthier team dynamics.

Lesson 7: Navigating Push back and Resistance

Emily's journey to redefining her availability included moments of push back and resistance from both colleagues and clients. Some clients expressed frustration when Emily did not respond to their emails immediately after hours, and a few colleagues made comments suggesting that she was not as committed as she used to be.

Initially, this push back made Emily doubt her decision to set boundaries. However, she reminded herself of the reasons why she needed to protect her well-being and maintain a healthier work-life balance. Emily responded to the push back by reiterating her commitment to providing high-quality work during regular hours and explaining how her boundaries allowed her to stay focused and effective.

Over time, Emily's consistency in maintaining her boundaries earned the respect of her colleagues and clients. They came to understand that her commitment to boundaries was not a reflection of diminished dedication, but rather a strategy for sustaining long-term productivity and well-being. Emily's experience highlights the importance of staying firm in one's boundaries, even in the face of resistance, and trusting that others will eventually adapt.

In conclusion, the real-life stories of professionals who have taken control of their work-life balance provide valuable insights into the challenges and rewards of maintaining boundaries. These case studies demonstrate that setting and maintaining boundaries is not a linear process—it involves ongoing reflection, adjustments, and the courage to assert one's needs in the face of resistance.

The lessons learned from failures and adjustments emphasize the importance of flexibility, open communication, and self-compassion. Boundaries are not about perfection; they are about creating guidelines that support well-being and fulfillment. By learning from these stories and embracing the journey of setting and maintaining boundaries, individuals can cultivate a healthier and more balanced approach to work and life.

Conclusion

Maintaining healthy boundaries between work, personal life, and self-care is essential for leading a balanced and fulfilling life. Consistently upholding these boundaries leads to numerous rewards, including improved well-being, stronger relationships, and enhanced productivity. Additionally, the impact of boundary-setting extends beyond the individual—it has the potential to influence future generations by creating a legacy of balanced living that values self-respect, emotional health, and thoughtful prioritization. This chapter explores the rewards of consistently upholding boundaries and discusses how individuals can create a legacy of balanced living for future generations.

The Rewards of Consistently Upholding Boundaries

The process of establishing and maintaining boundaries can be challenging, especially in environments or cultures that may not initially support them. However, the benefits of consistently upholding boundaries are profound and far-reaching. When boundaries are respected and integrated into daily life, individuals experience improvements in their physical health, mental clarity, emotional stability, and overall quality of life.

One of the most immediate rewards of upholding boundaries is the reduction of stress and burnout. Without clear boundaries, it's easy to become overwhelmed by competing demands from work, family, and social obligations. This constant juggling leads to chronic stress, which negatively impacts physical health, mental well-being, and relationships. By setting and maintaining boundaries, individuals can create a sense of order and predictability in their lives, allowing them to manage stress more effectively.

Boundaries also contribute to improved mental clarity and focus. When individuals establish clear limits around work tasks, personal commitments, and leisure activities, they can devote their full attention to each aspect of their lives without feeling pulled in multiple directions. For example, someone who sets boundaries around checking work emails after hours can fully engage in personal activities without the distraction of work-related concerns. This improved focus leads to higher productivity during work hours and more meaningful connections in personal interactions.

Emotional stability is another significant reward of consistently upholding boundaries. Boundaries protect individuals from becoming overly entangled in others' emotions or feeling responsible for others' well-being. This emotional separation allows individuals to experience empathy and compassion without compromising their own emotional health. For instance, someone who sets boundaries around being available for work-related issues during personal time can engage with colleagues empathetically during work hours while maintaining emotional distance outside of those hours.

Consistently upholding boundaries also leads to stronger and more fulfilling relationships. When individuals communicate their needs and limits openly and assertively, they establish a foundation of mutual respect and understanding in their relationships. This transparency prevents misunderstandings, resentment, and conflicts, allowing relationships to thrive. Additionally, when individuals uphold their own boundaries, they model healthy behavior for others, encouraging a culture of respect and self-care.

Another key reward of maintaining boundaries is the opportunity for personal growth and self-discovery. Setting boundaries requires self-awareness, assertiveness, and resilience, which are essential qualities for personal development. As individuals practice these skills, they gain a deeper understanding of their values, priorities, and aspirations. This self-knowledge enables them to make decisions that align with their authentic selves, leading to a greater sense of fulfillment and purpose.

Physical health is also positively impacted by upholding boundaries. Chronic stress, overwork, and burnout can take a significant toll on the body, leading to sleep disturbances, weakened immune function, and increased risk of illness. By setting boundaries around work hours, rest, and self-care, individuals can protect their physical health and maintain the energy needed to pursue their goals and enjoy their lives.

Financial well-being is another often-overlooked reward of boundary-setting. Clear boundaries around spending, saving, and investing help individuals make intentional financial decisions that align with their long-term goals and values. This financial clarity reduces stress and anxiety related to money, enabling individuals to build a stable foundation for themselves and their families.

Beyond these individual rewards, consistently upholding boundaries contributes to the creation of a balanced and fulfilling life. When individuals set limits that protect their time, energy, and well-being, they create the conditions for a life that is intentional, meaningful, and aligned with their values. This balanced approach allows individuals to pursue their passions, nurture their relationships, and achieve their goals without sacrificing their well-being.

Creating a Legacy of Balanced Living for Future Generations

The impact of consistently upholding boundaries extends beyond the individual—it has the potential to create a legacy of balanced living for future generations. By modeling healthy boundary-setting practices and promoting a culture of balance, individuals can influence their families, communities, and workplaces in ways that have lasting effects. This legacy is not only about the choices made today but also about the values and principles that are passed down to future generations.

One of the most powerful ways to create a legacy of balanced living is to model healthy boundaries for children and younger generations. Children learn by observing the behavior of the adults around them, and they are deeply influenced by the values and priorities that are demonstrated in their families and communities. When adults set and maintain clear boundaries around work, personal time, and self-care, they teach children the importance of respecting their own needs and limits.

For example, a parent who sets boundaries around working hours and prioritizes family time communicates the message that relationships and well-being are just as important as professional success. This modeling helps children develop a balanced perspective on work and life, reducing the likelihood of internalizing the belief that constant productivity and sacrifice are necessary for success.

In addition to modeling healthy behavior, adults can actively teach younger generations about the importance of boundaries. This teaching can take the form of conversations about the value of self-care, the importance of saying no when necessary, and the benefits of prioritizing well-being. For instance, parents can encourage their children to set boundaries around screen time, study time, and social activities to promote a balanced lifestyle. By having open discussions about boundaries, adults help children develop the skills and confidence needed to assert their needs and limits as they grow.

Beyond the family unit, creating a legacy of balanced living involves promoting a culture of balance in workplaces and communities. This requires challenging cultural norms that prioritize constant availability, overwork, and sacrifice at the expense of well-being. Leaders and managers play a crucial role in shaping workplace culture by modeling healthy boundaries, encouraging time off, and recognizing the value of rest and recovery.

For example, leaders who respect their own work hours and refrain from sending emails after hours set a powerful example for their teams. They communicate the message that boundaries are respected and that well-being is valued. This culture of balance not only benefits individual employees but also leads to greater productivity, creativity, and job satisfaction within the organization.

Creating a legacy of balanced living also involves advocating for systemic changes that support boundary-setting practices. This advocacy can take the form of promoting policies that encourage flexible work hours, mental health support, parental leave, and work-from-home options. By pushing for these changes, individuals and organizations can create environments that prioritize well-being and allow for the integration of work and personal life.

Community involvement is another key aspect of creating a legacy of balanced living. Engaging in community activities, volunteering, and supporting local initiatives promotes a sense of connection and purpose beyond work and individual pursuits. These activities provide opportunities to model balanced living and contribute to the well-being of others, reinforcing the message that a fulfilling life involves giving back and supporting one's community.

Creating a legacy of balanced living also requires ongoing reflection and commitment. It's important to recognize that the journey to balanced living is not linear or static—it involves continuous learning, adaptation, and growth. Life circumstances, responsibilities, and priorities will inevitably change over time, and boundaries must evolve to reflect these changes. By embracing this dynamic approach, individuals can remain resilient in the face of challenges and stay aligned with their values.

To pass on the legacy of balanced living to future generations, individuals must also recognize and challenge the internal and external pressures that undermine boundaries. This includes addressing societal expectations that equate success with constant busyness, pushing back against perfectionism, and rejecting the notion that self-care is selfish. By questioning these cultural messages and embracing a balanced approach, individuals can create a more compassionate and sustainable way of living.

Another aspect of creating a legacy of balanced living is cultivating self-awareness and emotional intelligence. These qualities are essential for understanding one's needs, recognizing when boundaries are being compromised, and making intentional choices. Individuals who cultivate self-awareness are better equipped to navigate challenges, build resilience, and maintain balance in the face of adversity.

In conclusion, consistently upholding boundaries leads to numerous rewards, including improved well-being, stronger relationships, and greater fulfillment. By creating a legacy of balanced living, individuals can positively influence future generations and contribute to a culture that values self-respect, emotional health, and intentional living. This legacy is not just about setting limits—it's about creating a life that prioritizes well-being, honors one's values, and supports the growth and flourishing of oneself and others.

A life of balance and fulfillment is within reach for those who are willing to embrace the journey of boundary-setting, self-reflection, and intentional living. By consistently upholding boundaries and creating a legacy of balanced living, individuals can lead lives that are not only successful but also deeply meaningful and aligned with their true selves.

www.ingramcontent.com/pod-product-compliance
Lightning Source LLC
Chambersburg PA
CBHW070425240526
45472CB00020B/1328